Stop Your Ticking Time Bomb Now!

The Ultimate Guide to Mastering Stress

and

Growing in Health and Happiness

Roseli Schmidt

The advice and information contained in this book are considered to be precise and correct at press time. The publisher and the author cannot accept any legal responsibility for any misunderstanding, error or negligence that may have been made.

The publisher does not promote the use of any particular healthcare protocol but believes that this content should be accessible to the public. The publisher and the author are not responsible for any adverse effects resulting from the use of the recommendations, preparations or ideas discussed in this book. If the reader has any questions relating to the information mentioned in this book, the author and the publisher strongly suggest you to consult a healthcare professional.

First edition published 2016 by RSR Publications

RSR Publications

London- England

E2 0QD

Associated companies throughout the world

www.rsrpublications.net

Copyright © Roseli Schmidt 2015

The right of Roseli Schmidt to be identified as the author of this work has been asserted by her in accordance with the Copyright, Designs and Patents Act 1988.

All rights reserved. No part of this publication may be reproduced, stored in or introduced into a retrieval system, or transmitted, in any form, or by any means (electronic, mechanical, photocopying, recording or otherwise) without the prior written permission of the publisher. Any person who does any unauthorized act about this publication may be liable to criminal prosecution and civil claims for damages.

Roseli's photo © 2016 Pellier Noir

Front cover images © 2016 Depositphotos Inc.

ISBN: 978-0-9955014-0-9

Dedications

To God be all the glory, honour, and praise.

In memory of Gerda Schmidt
You left your fingerprints of kindness and grace on me.

To my wonderful sons - you are my absolute joy! You two have inspired and supported me in reaching for the stars.

Support Your Local Charity

10% of all author royalties are donated to **Brain Tumour Research Campaign**

www.wayahead-btrc.org

Endorsements

I met Roseli Schmidt some years ago. I was impressed with her words, full of wisdom, compassion and love, and that inspired and transformed me. Her words changed my life forever. She is an angel in the earth!

Cledeir Goular – Sao Paulo- Brazil

I have often found profound reassurance in the wise counsel of Roseli Schmidt. I am glad that she has decided to demonstrate her knowledge in such an original book. I am confident that others will now be able to draw as much great inspiration from her words and thoughts as I have.

Gregory Patton - London- England

I was at a crossroads in my life, looking for a career change when I met Roseli for the first time. Roseli inspired and encouraged me so much. She is a strong very knowledgeable individual; there are no doubts about her success.

Naz Najeeb- Councillor & Student of Psychology -London- England

Roseli is a woman with an enviable courage. She works hard. She taught me so many things, and the best advice I received on this world came from her. She always inspires and encourages people to fight until achieving their goals.

Silvio Barbosa-Business Man- Santa Maria da Serra- Brazil

Roseli is a great woman, full of faith, courage and persistence. She is an inspiration for those who dream achieving higher goals.

Claudia Guimaraes- Special Needs Teacher- Sao Paulo- Brazil

I'm feeling so lucky for having the chance to read this book. It's definitely a book that I would suggest to my friends to read, and buy as a gift to someone. I loved it and I'm going to adapt its advice in my daily life, foremost the nutritional ones.

My mother has been diagnosed with depression and I've already started to try to find ways to adjust her diet according to all these amazing things I've learnt from this book.

And because I have troubled sleep, I think the chapter talking about sleep is my favourite chapter. And I think this book might already have changed my life.

Hermione Bloomsbury - Journalist – Athens- Greece

Roseli is one of the most incredible women I've ever met. Exemplary mother, devoted friend and a wonderful person. She is an enlightened person who manages to give the world a great charisma and companionship. She does everything with love, competence and excellence.

Dr. Elisa Mitie- Medical Doctor – London- England

Table of Contents

Acknowledgments *8*
Introduction *11*
The Paradox of Our Age *15*

UNDERSTANDING STRESS, AND ITS CONSEQUENCES ON YOUR HEALTH ..**17**
   CHAPTER 1 The Scary Truth in a Hyper Productive Society *19*
   CHAPTER 2 Stress Can Have Psychological Implications *25*
   CHAPTER 3 Quick Fixes *31*
   CHAPTER 4 Dangerous Paradise *41*

THE ACTION PLAN AGAINST STRESS **51**
   CHAPTER 5 Taking Out the Trash *53*
   CHAPTER 6 Only the Best for You *65*
   CHAPTER 7 Building Blocks for the Best Health *73*
   CHAPTER 8 Extra Strengths *93*
   CHAPTER 9 Right to Dream *105*
   CHAPTER 10 Exercise: The Easy Pill for Happiness *117*
   CHAPTER 11 Seeing in the Darkness *127*
   CHAPTER 12 Anaesthesia for the Pain *137*
   CHAPTER 13 The Gain From the Pain *147*
   CHAPTER 14 The Power of Love *169*

Contacting the Author *180*
Useful Websites *181*
Brain Tumour Research Campaign *183*
INDEX *185*
BIBLIOGRAPHY *186*

Acknowledgments

If I have seen further than others, it is by standing upon the shoulders of giants.
~ *Isaac Newton*

This quote reflects how I feel about those who have influenced my life. Many men and women full of determination, courage, thirst for knowledge and wisdom have been my inspiration up to this point. However, some of them I need to name. They are:

Professor Neide R. Nass, who taught me how to love psychology with all my heart.

Professor Maria Jose M. D. P. Mora, who blessed me with her knowledge, kindness and love.

Dr. Max Gerson, (Gerson Therapy), a Nobel Prize winner for his discovery of a natural cure for cancer.

Dr. Charlotte Gerson for sharing with the world her father's works.

Dr. Linus Pauling, another Nobel Prize winner, who discovered the use of nutrients in large doses to heal in psychiatric treatments.

Professor Dr. Lair Ribeiro, who has diligently studied and is freely teaching thousands of people, including me, the importance of good nutrition for the prevention of disease.

Siobhan Markwell, I'll never forget your eyes of love teaching me. You are the best English teacher I have ever met.

Richard Wills, who is the angel on my shoulder, always believing in me and thinking I am capable of achieving anything.

Elisa Kajita and **Romualdo Marcilio** for their support, especially through challenging times. I am very lucky to have both of you in my life.

Thank you to all. I am forever grateful.

Introduction

The things you do impact your well-being and your health. You may be doing things that are harming you without knowing it. Many people just realise something is going wrong when things seem to be out of control. When this happens, it's easy to become even more worried, anxious, sleepless and ill.

In the modern world, the word *busy* becomes the surname of most people. Moreover, to protect ourselves from the effects of bad stress, we need information about how to identify the early signals of stress and stop them with interventions to promote good health.

Now and moving into the future, information is the most precious treasure available in this world. Information is the door, and the key is our ability to access it, to digest the wisdom and to practice it routinely.

I experienced Post-Traumatic Stress Disorder and many other problems triggered by the sudden death of my mother. I was just twenty years old when I started struggling with severe depression that was slowly destroying my dreams and hopes, and bringing me uncertainty about the meaning of life and the worth of my presence in this world.

I admitted to myself that I had a problem and I sought help. However, even having visited many doctors and taking dozens of medications, the pain in my soul was great. The sensation of insignificance was growing fast, as were my thoughts of dying to reduce the pain. It became my only source of hope. I know this sounds controversial. However, when you are facing a severe mental illness, nothing makes sense and you feel so exhausted and lonely, fighting against your own thoughts. You don't see much reason to exist and you just want to give up.

As I tried to get better, sleeping pills and pills to stay awake became a daily part of my routine. I thought it was the only path toward seeing the beauty of life again and getting my life back. I was disciplined in taking those pills. However, instead of getting better, I found myself stuck in a nightmare that lasted almost a decade with a cocktail of medications that somewhat alleviated some symptoms of my depression, but never cured me. Then I got tired of being tired, and I started educating myself as a last attempt to climb out from that situation once and for all.

I admit that I fell many times. However, I didn't give up and, in the end, I won that terrible battle and I felt great and completely healed. Once more, after many years, I forgot to pay attention to myself so I had recurrent depression when my marriage finished and I faced divorce. I had a mild depression, but it still took me time and effort to get better. I won again and these days, life is brighter than ever!

From my experiences, I learned that no matter what, life is worth embracing and the power to overcome any situation is inside of you and me. All the answers are in us; we just need the right tools to access them.

When I read the tragic news about Robin Williams, I realised that it was time to open my mouth and share my knowledge and experiences with the world. But how would I do that? So, I wrote this book to reach more people.

This book is scientifically based on the fields of psychology, medicine and nutrition; this illustrates that we can prevent, treat and cure diseases in a natural way, with no need of traditional remedies.

Introduction

In this book, I share what I've learnt over the past twenty years. My knowledge comes from my own experiences, my continuous studies of thousands of books that I have read over the years, my academic degrees, and from assisting thousands of people who have crossed my path.

So, it is time for you learn how to protect yourself and those you love.

Please, share all the information you receive here; let's make it viral!

We need to keep talking and educating each other. There are so many anonymous Whitney Houstons and Robins Williamses around us suffering and dying. We must act now!

The lack of knowledge is still costing lives, destroying both our families and our society. It is time to fight against that and save lives.

The Paradox of Our Age

We have bigger houses and smaller families;
more conveniences, yet less time;
we have more degrees but less sense;
more knowledge but less judgement;
more experts, yet more problems;
. . . more medicine, yet less wellness . . . .
We've been all the way to the moon and back,
but have trouble crossing the street
to meet the new neighbour. . . .
We build more computers to hold more information,
to produce more copies than ever, but have less
communication;
We've become long on quantity,
but short on quality.
These are the times of fast foods
and slow digestion;
tall men, but short character;
steep in profits, but shallow relationships. . . .
It is a time when there is much in the show window
and nothing in the stock room.

~ Dr. Bob Moorehead

PART ONE

UNDERSTANDING STRESS, AND ITS CONSEQUENCES ON YOUR HEALTH

CHAPTER 1
The Scary Truth in a Hyper Productive Society

Come out of the masses. Stand alone like a lion and live your life according to your own light.
~Osho

Tens of thousands of years ago, we didn't know what to expect in the future, and we had no idea about the possibilities we would now have. Modern life is like a coin; it has two sides - one very good and one very bad. Modern life has immeasurably changed my life. Twenty years ago, I was working hard to get my first psychology degree. Because of that, I can say that I have had the chance to experience both the *old* and the *modern* times. Back then, I used to carry tons of books from the library with me to track down the information I needed. Now when I go to the university I don't need to carry any books. I just need a tablet and a good internet connection to access all the information I need.

Today, with the advent of the internet and its wide availability, learning has never been so easy. It now can be done anywhere, anytime. Google and YouTube are my preferred teachers. It is amazing; the enormous volumes of information the internet can bring to us is beyond what can be captured in any amount of books.

However, as I said before, making life easier is the good side of the coin. The bad side is that advanced technology is distracting us and it is contributing to us losing our focus on the environment and on ourselves. One good example of this is the mobile phone. It is so amazing when you think about how it makes it easy to talk with people far away, but the sad side of that is, it also can make you forget to talk with those who are physically close, beginning with family and friends. The "internet era" has brought the necessity of continually upgrading ourselves. The upgrading era is brimming with challenges, worries, deadlines, and guess what? It is time demanding because of the constant rush.

The eating habits of the majority of people today have changed for the worse. Look around your neighbourhood. Unfortunately, vast amount of fast food restaurants and junk food offers are still growing quickly, much like people's diseases.

It seems that humanity has been transformed into puppets, or has been hypnotized to behave without thinking about what they are doing. I really avoid junk foods. However, sometimes I see myself without any better option and I succumb to that, too. But I know that when I eat junk food, I am only filling my body with empty calories to get an immediate rush of energy. Nevertheless, I am not getting any nutrients that my body needs, but lots of what my body doesn't need, such as fat, sugar and sodium.

Unfortunately, many people don't realise this. They have turned into eating machines that pay little attention to what they're putting into their bodies. This lack of attention in relation to what foods to eat and what foods not to eat has brought serious consequences. Diseases such as obesity, high blood pressure, depression, diabetes, heart diseases, autoimmune diseases and many other degenerative diseases have become increasingly prevalent.

The old times won't return, and stress is everywhere. There is nothing you can do about this. The good news is that you can change your response to it, protecting yourself by identifying the signs and symptoms of stress and taking early actions to reduce its destructive effects on your health and wellbeing.

In small amounts, stress is good because it can provide you with the motivation you need to achieve certain tasks, even when you are under pressure. However, when you're continuously operating in *emergency mode*, your mind and body pay the price. Unfortunately, stress has become a common state of mind for many people.

What is Stress?

Stress is a typical response to events or circumstances when you feel threatened or in danger (Csikszentmihalyi, 1999). As soon as you sense danger, whether real or imaginary, your body's defence mechanism will enter into *combat mode,* also known as the fight-or-flight response (Caspi, 2003). When feeling danger, your body's defence mechanism increases your focus, energy levels, and alertness.

The positive aspect of stress is that it gives you extra strength, making you rise above your expectations and helping you deal with challenges in a more efficient manner. For example, stress might motivate you to keep studying for your exams instead of watching TV or resting.

However, when you reach a certain point, stress loses its beneficial properties. Instead, it leads to negative consequences in your body, such as chemical imbalances that can cause changes to your humour, weight fluctuations, aging and chronic diseases.

The Body's Response to Stress

Research has shown that the brain and the nervous system respond to stress in three different ways. According to Dr Jeanne Segal and colleagues (on the website www.helpguide.org), they are:

1. **Social communication,** or social engagement, is what people use the most when we want to calm down and feel safe.

   Opinions differ on this. Some people say that they don't feel comfortable when they are with others. In my view, it will depend on the quality of friends you have around you, and the relationship you have with them. Considering that you feel safe around your friends, the face-to-face interaction of talking, attentive listening and eye contact helps you slow down the fight-or-flight response. It is easy to help others calm down using this strategy; it has been extensively used by people because asking others for help or forgiveness can quickly clean up misinterpretations, ensuring healthy and strong social interactions.

   Real connection by social interaction helps the body regulate better involuntary functions such as blood pressure, respiratory activity, heart rate and digestion, working healthily to restore and continuously produce new cells. Now you know why a big hug is so powerful. I recommend that you increase the number of hugs and make them part of your daily routine.

2. **Mobilization,** also known as the fight-or-flight response, usually happens when social engagement isn't available or isn't the most appropriate option. In this case, when you feel threatened, stress works as a great help by providing you a burst of energy that is required to defend yourself in a fight or to run away

CHAPTER 1: The Scary Truth in a Hyper productive Society

from danger. A good example for that is to imagine a tiger roaring in front of you. In a real scenario, when you see the tiger, stress hormones are instantly released to arouse the body to take action.

In this situation, your sympathetic nervous system produces an adrenal secretion of epinephrine, which is helpful in warming up your body and preparing it to run or fight. Whenever this happens, an increase of heart rate and blood flows to the brain and muscles rapidly. This also causes shallow breath, sweat on hands and the soles of feet, pupil dilatation and a sudden increase of blood sugar levels to increase energy.

These physical alterations boost your strength and stamina and also improve your concentration, speed up your reaction time, and sharpen your senses such as smell, vision, and hearing. When this occurs, bodily functions that are not engaged in the fight-or-flight scenario slow down momentarily. For example, your digestive as well as immune systems cease operating and slow down the maintenance and growth of tissues inside the body.

As soon as the danger is gone, your nervous system sends a message to your body and it starts calming down until it returns to the pre-stress balance.

3. **Immobilization** occurs when the first two responses have been unsuccessful or inappropriate. It usually appears when people are experiencing some distress and find themselves feeling *stuck*. The fears turn into a destructive and panic-stricken state of mind. This normally occurs in Post-Traumatic Stress Disorder.

   In this situation, people feel like the *scenario* doesn't allow them to move on with their lives. As a result, the nervous system stops operating properly and the person living in this situation may experience periodic or ongoing decreased functionality.

Being exposed to an extreme situation can result in the loss of consciousness or collapse as a way to help the person to survive significant levels of physical pain. Nevertheless, the nervous system will not be able to return to the pre-stress state of equilibrium until it becomes capable of arousing the body to a mobilization or fight-or-flight state.

Your body can display external signs of stress in two categories:

- In *fight* mode you may feel overactive; this leads you to feel anger, and/or agitation, to overreact and/or sit still.
- In *flight* mode you may feel low levels of energy and low-spirited, resulting in isolation and depression.

The flight mode also presents the same signals when you experience immobilization or frozen stress response. This means that on the outside you may look stagnated while internally you feel nervous and hopeless.

CHAPTER 2

Stress Can Have Psychological Implications

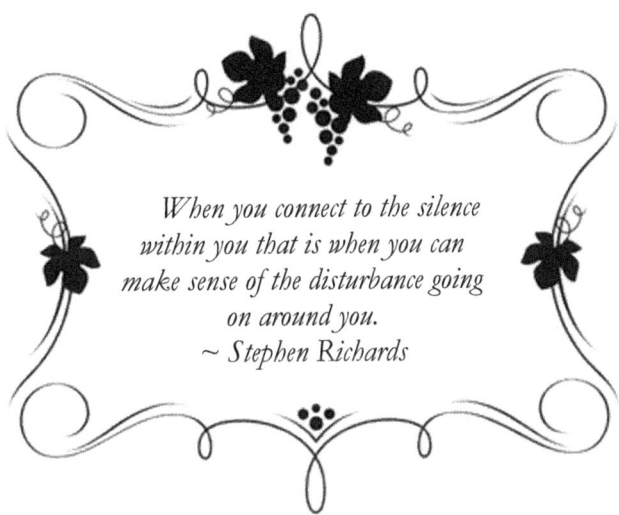

When you connect to the silence within you that is when you can make sense of the disturbance going on around you.
~ Stephen Richards

Stress tolerance levels differ from person to person, and there is no known way to determine how much stress is actually *too much* for you. The explanation may be simple: as a person, you are unique! While some people can easily adapt to imposed changes and go with the flow, others seem to fall apart as soon as they stumble upon new problems or frustrations.

Your capacity to tolerate stress comes from many factors. Healthy eating choices and an invigorating and restorative sleep can greatly increase your level of stress tolerance.

I strongly believe this, and I am going to expand more on these topics in Chapters 6 and 9.

It is very important that you understand that other psychological and medical issues can trigger symptoms of diseases. Because of this, it is vital to pay attention to the signals your body is giving to you and consult with your health care provider for a full check-up if you're observing any warning signs.

The following list presents some indicators of high levels of stress. The more signs you identify, the more pronounced the problem of stress overload might be.

- Chronic Worry
- Feeling Anxious (inability to relax)
- Moodiness
- Racing Thoughts
- Difficulty Concentrating
- Memory Issues
- Rigid Thinking (All-or-nothing attitude)
- Feeling Melancholic
- Loneliness

The above symptoms are cognitive and emotional symptoms, and they also can provoke physical symptoms such as:

- Cardiac Arrhythmia
- Weakened Immune System (frequent allergies and flus)
- Loss of Libido
- Constipation or Diarrhoea
- Pains
- Nausea and Vomiting
- Frequent Urination
- Tremors and Twitches
- Shortness of Breath
- Muscle Tension
- Exhaustion
- High/ Low Blood Pressure

Other symptoms of chronic stress are:

- Unhealthy Coping Habits (caffeine, cigarettes, drugs, etc.)
- Procrastination
- Isolation
- Perfectionism
- Appetite Loss or Gain
- Insomnia or Sleeping Too Much
- Nervous Habits (biting nails or lower lip, chewing things such as pencils or pens, pulling or touching hair, etc.)

As discussed in the previous chapter, chronic stress can have a negative impact on your entire body. Prolonged stress usually affects blood pressure and weakens the immune system. It can also trigger other health problems such as infertility and enhance the risk of having a stroke or heart attack, which can affect the person's life expectancy and lead to premature death. Constant stress experienced over a long period can speed up the aging process, which can result in chronic diseases such as diabetes and cancer.

Regrettably, stress also can have psychological implications, such as chronic anxiety.

Anxiety is far more than an emotion and includes an array of physical symptoms that normally differ from person to person. While one person might go through intense anxiety attacks with minimal problems, another person can get scared just by thinking of interacting with people at a party. Someone else may be subjected to constant tension, worrying about practically everything in their daily lives. For these reasons, those who suffer from anxiety are sometimes misdiagnosed; their symptoms may be confused with other medical illnesses. They might end up consulting lots of health specialists and having tons of check-ups until they understand that their health issue is a symptom of an anxiety disorder.

According to the Anxiety and Depression Association of America (ADAA), anxiety comes in six major forms, and knowing what you have can help you better manage it. Each of the six major types has a specific symptom profile, with some overlapping signs and symptoms. The forms include Generalised Anxiety Disorder (GAD), Obsessive-Compulsive Disorder (OCD), Panic Disorder (anxiety attacks), Phobias, Post-Traumatic Stress Disorder and Social Anxiety Disorder.

http://www.adaa.org/understanding-anxiety

1 - General Anxiety Disorder (GAD)

GAD usually manifests as constant fears and worries or a persistent feeling that something bad is about to occur. Those who experience GAD feel constant anxiety, sometimes without being aware of the reasons. Physical symptoms that accompany this condition are insomnia, indigestion, agitation and exhaustion.

2 - Obsessive Compulsive Disorder (OCD)

OCD involves uncontrollable or intrusive thoughts or behaviours that are practically uncontrollable. Those who deal with OCD experience obsessions (for example, a constant worry or concern that you may have forgotten to lock the door). You may also feel subjected to strong compulsions, such as washing your hands repeatedly.

3 - Panic Disorder

Anxiety can lead to panic attacks; these may come unexpectedly and without warning (Hagnell, 1982). At times, there is a clear trigger, such as being trapped in a lift or worrying about an impending speech. In others cases, the attacks occur unexpectedly. They come accompanied by the worry or fear of going through another episode soon. One of the associated conditions is agoraphobia, the phobia that you might be at a location where help is not available. In the majority of cases, those who deal with agoraphobia avoid public areas such as shopping centres or restricted spaces such as an airplane.

4 - Phobias

Phobias are unrealistic fears of things that normally are not threatening. Some of the typical phobias are fears of spiders, snakes, heights or flying. Many people practice avoidance if they experience a certain type of phobia. However, in the majority of cases, avoidance only reinforces the phobia. I will expand on this in Chapter 11.

5 - Post-Traumatic Stress Disorder (PTSD)

PTSD usually occurs as a response to a traumatic event such as a terrorist attack, natural disaster, unexpected death or loss of a loved one, rape, car or plane crash, physical abuse, war, assault, childhood neglect or kidnapping.

Those experiencing PTSD may have nightmares or memories of previous events. They tend to isolate themselves, trying to avoid events that might relate to the past dreadful occurrences they have been subjected to (Courtois, 2009).

In my case, I experienced PTSD as a response to the unexpected death of my mother. During that time, my life was frenetic and overwhelming. Many things were happening at the same time. You will read more about my story in Chapter 13.

6 - Social Anxiety Disorder (SAD)

SAD, or social phobia, is a terrible worry or fear of being negatively received or humiliated in public. Sometimes this can be associated with intense shyness. When social phobia escalates, sufferers try to avoid social situations.

As you can see, anxiety disorders have different forms. However, there is one common symptom present in all conditions: the sensation of severe or constant fear, worry or threat in scenarios that normally present no danger at all.

CHAPTER 3

Quick Fixes

*Sensitive people suffer more, but
they love more and dream more.*
~Augusto Cury

Stress can make you feel sick mentally and/or physically, especially when it accumulates on a daily basis. In contrast to stress, depression is the result of unrelenting stress. When you are unable to manage stressful conditions over a period of time, you may feel restless and unable to control your life. For example, when you feel unable to cope with your job or other situations in your life, you may be experiencing a state of depression.

In others words, *depression* is an imbalance between the psychological, physical and the emotional, caused by exhaustion (Caspi A. K., 2003). This imbalance is provoked by chemical imbalance within the body. Organs such as the liver, pancreas, thyroid, gut and adrenals start having trouble working properly. When one or more organs cannot perform, other organs will be overwhelmed. The body starts accumulating more toxins, and the most sensitive organ to suffer with this situation is the brain.

When you are experiencing depression, the accumulation of toxins and the decreased functioning of some organs may make you feel resentful, miserable and apathetic. There is no motivation to push yourself and you withdraw from the world. Depression normally leads to low productivity. Apart from having a psychological impact, long-term depression can deteriorate physical health. For example, your immune system decreases, which in turn makes you more susceptible to other illnesses.

The following points will clarify the significant differences between depression and stress.

Stress	Depression
Agitation	Detachment
Overactive Emotions	Decreased Emotions
Sense of Urgency	Helplessness
Lack of Energy	Lack of Ideas, Incentive and Hope
Anxiety Disorders	Disinterest
Starts with Physical Symptoms	Starts with Emotional Symptoms
Increases the Risk to Develop Chronic Illness and It May Decrease Your Life Expectance	Feeling that Life Seems Worthless

The following points further clarify the relationship between stress and depression:

- Stress involves being excessively engaged by multiple pressures or demands; on the other hand, a depressed person wants disconnection. There is a feeling of emptiness.

- The stressed person shows more emotions (for example: cries easily and sometimes over-exaggerates), whereas a mildly or moderately depressed person shows sadness, sense of guilt and/or remorse and helplessness. However, when the person is experiencing severe depression the person shows indifferent, completely apathetic.

- Stress first reflects as physical symptoms, which gradually affects emotional health. On the other hand, depression affects emotions first.

- Stress makes the person feel drained (because they feel the urge to do more); depression involves lack of incentive, ideas and hope.

- Stressed people know they are under stress, and they try to find ways to deal with it. However, depressed people don't always notice when the depression is occurring.

My experience has shown me that less than 10% of children grow up in a healthy and safe environment that gives them the feeling of being loved and protected. Anxiety and depression are physical and emotional symptoms that appear when the soul is hurt by memories; *bad* words received and aborted dreams that has generated frustrations. Usually, a person who is suffering from anxiety and depression is bringing inside of her/him an emotional heavy load with roots that came from childhood. Frequently this person comes from a toxic environment or *sick home*. I call a sick home a home where the environment predominantly offers the child some bad models such as fears, excessive control, insecurities, abuse (physical and verbal), excess responsibility at a young age and the absence of healthy relationships between family members. All these scenarios create memories of fears, angers, remorse stored in the part of the brain called the amygdala (Ehrlich, 2009). When those accumulated negative feelings are unresolved inside the person, it can turn into stress and depression.

Sometimes the symptoms of stress and depression overlap. You may not realise when you cross the blurred line between these conditions. Most of us do not even realise when we are in a depressive state. Therefore, dealing with stress or depression requires identifying the symptoms to recognise the condition in the first place. Once you are aware of the warning signs and symptoms, you can take the necessary steps to deal with the problem.

Some of the common signs and indicators of stress and depression can be seen through behaviour. There is behaviour considered normal in society that is indicative of acute stress or depression and can be considered *destructive pain management*. The most common behaviours I want to highlight include:

Smoking

Do you smoke more cigarettes when you are under stress? Many people resort to smoking to deal with day-to-day stress. Ask some smokers and they'll tell you smoking gives them pleasure and relieves their worries. However, studies have found that rather than help smokers relax, because of the nicotine and others stimulant substances, smoking increases anxiety and tension. Hence, a vicious circle that easily causes dependency. According to specialists on the subject, cigarettes have more than 400 substances, 43 being carcinogenic (cancer causing) chemical substances. Smoking has a huge impact on health. Cigarettes are also expensive, so they dig a hole in your pocket, too. In addition, smoking, binge drinking, drugs consume etc. are considered a self-harm behaviour without lethal intent.

Alcohol

Alcoholism starts casually as a way to de-stress the mind or enjoy a social gathering. Before the drinker realises it, this occasional or recreational use can ultimately lead to alcohol addiction. The condition becomes so severe that the drinker feels a compulsive need to drink alcohol in large quantities, which in turn results in several physical and psychological effects on health. According to substance abuse experts, alcohol abuse is different from alcoholism. Alcohol abusers know their limits on alcohol intake and can stop drinking if they do not feel

CHAPTER 3: Quick Fixes

well. On the other hand, because of dependency, alcoholics cannot simply stop drinking.

The effects of alcohol abuse or alcoholism on health are well known. Abuse of alcohol for an extended duration can affect the heart, liver and immune system. This dangerous and devastating condition can have an extensive negative impact not just on the victim, but also on people close to them. It can seriously affect the user's life socially, financially and psychologically.

Alcohol addiction can be an overwhelming experience for the user and his family. The best way to deal with it is by identifying the triggering stress factors. Once the drinker has the tools to effectively handle stress, he will be able to wean off drinking. The website www.smartrecovery.org offers lots of information to help alcohol abusers and their family handle the stress and quit alcohol through therapy.

Recreational Prescription Drugs

Some prescription pills like sleeping pills, painkillers, etc. have mild relaxing effects on the mind. Each year, more people are using recreational pills to relax. Many people take these pills to beat stress occasionally. These medicines relax and de-stress the mind, numbing the brain and temporarily reducing pain, anxiety and frustration. However, these medicines do not act on the root of the problem and do not provide a solution to stress or depression.

Although relying on an occasional pill for a quick fix may seem innocent enough, it can lead the user to develop a compulsive need (dependency) to take these recreational or prescription pills which may increase the risk for several physical and psychological effects (Keers, 2012). When taken for a long duration, these drugs can cause permanent damage to vital organs like the liver and brain and can affect life expectancy.

Caffeine or Other Energy Drinks

Who doesn't like a good cup of coffee? Many individuals turn to caffeine or energy drinks to beat fatigue and tiredness after a poor night's sleep or to help face a busy schedule. However, this can turn into a dependency. Many of us turn the kettle on to start the day with a morning cup of coffee. Nevertheless, very few of us know that this pick-me-up can also be harmful when taken in large quantities.

Caffeine immediately boosts your mental as well as physical alertness, and you feel active and energetic. However, as soon as the caffeine effect wears off, your body and mind feel even more tired and start craving another cup. The continuous use of caffeine makes you feel restless and disturbs your sleep. Consequently, you feel discouraged and lethargic on the next day (Lane, 1990).

Some people don't know they are intolerant or allergic to caffeine. Caffeine intolerance can present physical and psychological indications such as agitation, nervousness, anxiety, schizophrenia and psychoses (Clementz & Dailey, 1988).

Caffeine also acts as a diuretic, which means it increases urination. Many caffeine fans present dehydration signals without noticing.

If you think the decaffeinated version is the healthy option, you are completely wrong. Decaffeinated coffee can be more dangerous to your health than caffeinated drinks because it contains toxic solvents like benzene, chloroform or trichloroethylene.

Tips

To stop caffeine use, gradually start reducing the number of drinks. This allows your body to get accustomed to the lower levels and avoid withdrawal symptoms.

Avoid drinking coffee two hours before and two hours after meals because caffeine can disrupt the absorption of iron and vitamin C from the food.

Avoid using disposable coffee cups because the plastic material is made with Bisphenol-A (BPA). When the plastic cup receives hot liquid inside, the plastic contaminates the contents. Bisphenol-A is extremely toxic and detrimental to health (Vandenberg, 2007).

Food

High concentrations of hormones are produced in your body when you feel stressed. One of them, called cortisol, slows down your metabolism, causing you to store fat, accumulate toxins and retain liquids in your body. This causes more weight gain than you would normally experience. In addition, when you are facing stressful situations, you are using extra energy in your nervous system and muscles. This causes you to eat more than normal and crave more fatty, salty and sugary foods such as sweets and processed foods.

Scientists are considering that stress may be the reason why obesity is on the rise (Faith, 1997). According to their findings, people are too stressed and busy to cook their own food at home, thereby increasing the amount of fast food consumed.

Ice cream, cookies, chips and colas are devoid of nutrients and loaded with calories. Moreover, these foods do not help you to beat stress. In fact, the opposite holds true. A diet based on fast food will certainly make you very sick in a short period.

The best way to deal with a craving is filling your fridge and kitchen cabinets with healthier options. Therefore, even if you feel a craving for chewing due to stress or anxiety, you will eat healthy stuff. Also, try to find the cause of your stress and use the stress techniques suggested in this book to address your stress.

TV and Computer

Sitting in front of the television or computer for hours is a good way to lose yourself, even if it may seem like a fun way to beat stress.

Most people sit in front of the screen to avoid unwanted stressful situations and get lost in the virtual world. If this is the strategy you are using to escape real world situations, be forewarned that it can only provide momentary relief from worries and problems. However, when being online is more interesting or funny than real life interaction, there is a problem.

There are many apps that can help you control the time you spend online. Some apps such Rescue Time, Self-control and Freedom can help you monitor and reduce your online time.

I experienced the devastating effects of internet addiction in my home. My husband at the time presented all the symptoms of addiction such as lying and spending large amounts of time and money online. I tried many times to help him, but he never admitted to having internet problems. For him, spending fifteen hours a day in front of the TV playing online video games was a pleasure, not a problem. For me and my sons it was a big problem and because of this my eighteen years of marriage ended.

Suggestion:

Use TV or surfing the internet for a reasonable amount of time and with good reason; connecting with people by Skype or Meetup are just two examples of ways to connect with new and interesting people who share your interests. In addition, the internet can increase your research skills and your general knowledge. It can enrich your life and make you feel good about yourself.

Others tips are:

- Take breaks away from the computer, perhaps ten minutes each hour, to have a short walk outside, meditate or exercise.
- On the weekend try to meet real friends. Go camping, fishing, picnic or walk on the park without internet.
- In your time with family, friends, or your alone time, leave the phone at home or turn it off and put it in your pocket or bag.
- It is a good idea to practice a sport or your favourite hobby regularly.

Compulsive Spending

It's easy to feel tempted to buy unnecessary things when you are stressed; some people use compulsive spending as a way to cope with negative feelings or stress. The act of frivolous spending on arbitrary items may temporarily give you pleasant feelings. However, shopping to heal your emotional wounds may cause unintended consequences. This short-term pleasure can be followed by the pain of paying steep credit card bills.

The negative side of using cards and online shopping instead of paying by cash is that you don't feel like you are spending real money. Studies show that most people are less likely to buy, or are less enthusiastic to spend as much, when paying with cash instead of cards.

Compulsive shopping can start as a one-time mood booster, but be aware that it can soon grow into a compulsion. If you find yourself indulging in compulsive spending now and then to beat stress, maybe it is time to cultivate healthy habits to help you deal with stress in a more permanent way.

Examine what money means to you; try to notice how you interact with money and what attitudes and beliefs you have about money. Research shows that people with low self-esteem engage in more impulsive spending on the superficial (D' Astrous, 1990).

Remind yourself daily that money, the things it can pay for or the lack of it doesn't determine who you are or your value. You are very worthwhile as a person and it has nothing to do with the price of your clothes, mobile phone or how much money you have in your bank account. When you accept that as true, and money is no longer associated with your sense of self-worth, you pull down the psychological barriers that were keeping you from smart money management.

CHAPTER 4

Dangerous Paradise

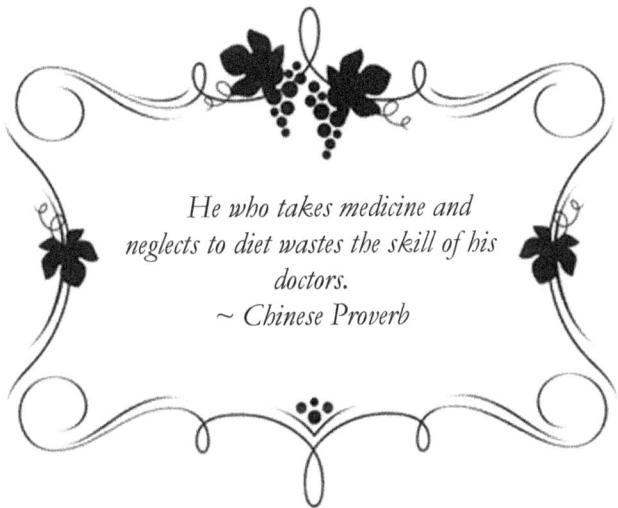

He who takes medicine and neglects to diet wastes the skill of his doctors.
~ Chinese Proverb

Toxins are harmful substances produced by a living organism (Sheldon, 1988). However, the word 'toxin' may refer to anything, be it synthetic or natural, that is poisonous. Toxins affect the body negatively and, in the worst-case scenario, can be fatal. The effects of some toxins may appear instantly and are transitory, while others need to build up to a particular level before they begin to show any prominent effects.

Depending on your lifestyle, the number of toxins your body receives will vary. An unhealthy lifestyle will certainly expose you to hundreds more toxins, compared to someone with a healthy one, and you will be more predisposed to disease than they will. Fortunately, our bodies have built-in detoxification systems with the power to combat toxins. These systems allow the body to detoxify itself on its own.

However, you must remember that while your body does an extraordinary job of fighting off toxins, if the exposure to these substances increases beyond its limits, your body may become overloaded with toxins.

Over time, your energy level can become impaired due to continued exposure to toxins. This can also affect your ability to concentrate and impair your immune system, too (Candance, 1997). As a result, you may experience conditions such as infections, allergies and constant flus, degenerative diseases, anxiety and so on.

As explained on Chapter 1, the accumulation of toxins provokes a chemical imbalance in the body. According to Dr Lair Ribeiro (cardiologist, psychiatrist and nutrition specialist), organs such as the liver, pancreas, thyroid, gut and adrenals works together, and they are the *door* for diseases. When one of them isn't working properly because of the accumulation of toxins or is affected by illness, others organs cannot perform at full potential, and the body starts accumulating even more toxins. The most sensitive organ to suffer from this is the brain.

It is important to learn about the primary sources of these harmful substances to minimize your exposure to toxins and protect yourself from their effects. Toxins can be found in many places. The most common are:

Foods

Food consumption is a primary source of toxins. The extent of harmful substances ingested will depend on the types of foods you eat. If your diet mainly consists of highly processed foods or the ingestion of artificial ingredients such as dyes, colourings, flavour enhancers and harmful artificial preservatives, you are exposing yourself to a considerable amount of toxins that require your body to work overtime to eliminate.

CHAPTER 4: Dangerous Paradise

Nevertheless, reducing the intake of unhealthy foods like sweets is just one of the many things that you need to do to fight against toxins. You must be aware that sugar is also present in various other foods, such as bread, canned foods, margarine, ketchup, etc.

Foods labelled as "low-fat" or "reduced fat" also have sugar in them. Food manufacturers replace fat with sugar to enhance the taste of some food items (Cannon, 2002). When you consume some foods that are high in sugar, you are only providing your body with empty calories. Sugar is recognised as an anti-nutrient, affecting the absorption of other nutrients in your body. This results in malnutrition, making your body vulnerable to diseases. In addition, overconsumption of foods high in sugar and/or simple carbohydrates cause inflammation, make your body sugar resistant, induce mood swings, accelerate the aging process and open the door to many diseases, including diabetes.

Did you know that soft drinks such as soda have lots of salt, preservatives, colours, flavours (acids) and sugar that may not be apparent? Isn't it shocking? Yes! It is true. However, let's talk just about the sugar. For example, a single can of Coke has 39g of sugar, resulting in around 140 calories.

You might think to switch to diet soda, but this only introduces other problems. Studies show that diet soda triggers cravings for sugar, which in turn can contribute to increasing your weight (Yang, 2010). Another thing worth remembering is that sugar is the villain that increases the acidity in your body. Because of this it increases the risk of cell mutation on the body. Sugar feeding cancer cells need an acidic environment to grow.

Maybe you are thinking that the best tasting foods in the world are forbidden on a healthy diet. Well, if they are full of fat, sugar and salt, they are. The American Heart Association (AHA) recommends no more that 24g of sugar a day for women and 36g a day for men. This means that only by consuming one can of soda you easily exceed the recommendation for sugar. In the UK, the food industry recommends the maximum intake should be 90g of sugar per day. It is worth remembering that apart from soda or artificial juice drinks, there are other foods that also contain sugar, such as fruits or milk. Some foods will turn into sugar in your body, such as grains, vegetables, milk and carbohydrates. So be careful!

However, if you want to consume sugar there are better options such as brown sugar, coconut sugar, stevia, molasses, demerara sugar or honey. These versions present some nutrients, of course. They vary according to the type of sugar, but they are much better than the common white refined sugar. The white refined sugar has been bleached with strong, dangerous chemicals, and all the nutrients is washed out on the bleaching process. Remember to use it in small quantities. It is better to give preference to organic versions.

The best approach to keep toxins down and health up is to be selective about what you eat, opting for fresh and, when possible, organic foods instead of processed foods.

Water

Drinking tap water will expose your body to numerous toxins. It has chemicals in it, such as fluoride or chlorine, which are added to control bacterial outbreaks. You'll also find other substances in your tap water such as aluminium, copper and mercury. Research also shows that some tap water sources contain traces of birth control medication and other prescription medications that are flushed down the toilet (WHO, 2011). The public falsely relies on the water treatment plants to clean up these harmful elements, but they do not.

It is your responsibility to check your own water quality. You can do this by checking the report on the web that comes from your water supplier to find the details of the contents of your tap water. Contaminants may also come from pipes in poor condition that trickle in lead. According to research, metal contaminants in the human body increase the risk for neurological disorders, such as Parkinson's and Alzheimer's (Connor, 1997).

Don't think by exchanging tap water for bottled mineral water you are avoiding toxins. Research has shown that water bottles also are a big source of water contamination. This is because of the plastic composition, such as Bisphenol-A (BPA). This kind of contamination is believed to be associated with many illness such as endocrine ailments, infertility, and degenerative diseases such as cancer (Peterson, 2010).

Toxins are more likely to drain into the bottle contents or container when using plastics. Those made with petroleum material are the worst offenders. When the plastic bottle is heated, (on the transport to the shop, before you buy it, or in your car in a sunny day) chemical substances migrate from the plastic into the water, thereby contaminating the drinking water. Exposing the bottle to sunlight or heating it in a microwave will increase the contamination. This reaction also occurs when inserting warm liquid contents in a baby's milk bottle. This process may also take place with acidic beverage contents (e.g., Coke).

It is shocking, but many chemicals in your water supply can transform into a gas when they are heated. For instance, you breathe chemicals directly into your lungs before they are absorbed into your blood while you take a shower, because of this, it's best to shower with filtered water; I advise you to purchase a shower filter. The same phenomenon happens when you use humid saunas. To avoid that just use a humid sauna treated by ozone, or a dry sauna instead.

If you wish to detoxify your body by drinking water, it is strongly recommended that you buy a quality water filter. The filter needs to remove all pollutants, impurities, chemicals and sediments from your tap water. However, the best filters are those that also have an additional system, which increases the pH, making your drinking water pure, alkaline and antioxidant.

Air

Air is another major source of toxins. The air you breathe in to survive is polluted. However, the number of toxins that you absorb from the air depends on various factors.

For example, if you are a resident of a large city or metropolitan area, you may be exposed to more air pollutants compared to others who are living in the countryside where there is less smoke from factories and less car traffic. There is not much you can do to minimize your exposure to harmful substances outdoors. People who live in Japan and China use facemasks; this is a common preventive practice to reduce toxin inhalation.

Other than the outdoor factors, pollution may also take place within your home. The chemicals that you use for various purposes, such as cleaning your house, or the chemicals that have fragrance such as hairspray, hair dye, perfumed candles, incenses, perfume and deodorant are also toxins.

Some studies have shown that indoor air has more toxins than outside air (Nasjikal, 2015). If you ventilate your home regularly through open windows and doors, you will considerably reduce toxic air inside your home. But there is more you can do to reduce the toxin levels inside your home. For example, you can avoid or limit the use of chemical sprays. If you have to use them, be sure to open a window to expel the harmful vapours from your home. In the same way, you need to limit or stop using liquid chemical products like surface cleaners. Smelling a product is no less safe than eating it. It may be as toxic as if you ingested it, so you need to be cautious!

CHAPTER 4: Dangerous Paradise

An air filter can make the air in your home fresher and healthier. You can place some live plants, such as aloe vera, spider plant, gerbera daisy, golden pothos, chrysanthemum and other species to filter the air. Any one of these has the ability to clear the air, especially from benzene. Some household products, such as detergent, plastic glue and paint, contain benzene. The bonus is that these plants beautify your home while cleaning the air in a natural way.

Your Lifestyle Choices Matter

In addition to the above information, if you are sedentary, your body will not be able to dispose of the harmful substances effectively. Your lymphatic system, one of your body's natural detoxification structures, needs movement to work efficiently. Because fat stores toxins, your percentage of body fat is directly related to your level of physical activity, which can gravely affect the amount of toxins you are storing. If you are overweight, then fat-soluble toxins will continue to affect your health until you can reduce your excess fat.

Electromagnetic Radiation

It is recommended that you also pay attention to Electromagnetic Radiation (EMR) and Microwave Radiation (MWR) created by electric and wireless devices and microwave ovens. Even though this radiation is not classified as *toxic*, you cannot ignore its ill effects.

All electronic devices release radiation. There are two types of radiation — the non-ionising radiation and the ionising radiation. The non-ionising form emits low energy radiation and it is found in some devices, such as microwaves ovens, radios, Wi-Fi (wireless internet connections), radar waves and mobile phones. The ionising radiation emits high-energy radiation and you can find that in medicine to treat or diagnose illness. The ionising radiation is found in X-rays, CT scans, radiotherapy (cancer treatment), and nuclear medicine.

Both forms of radiation accumulate in the body and can damage your cells, especially the ionising form. However, some studies reveal the possibility that devices, such as mobile phones and wireless routers, may cause damage to all parts of the brain including the hippocampus, the brain's memory centre. Exposure can cause mood and behavioural changes, or even worse, can have adverse effects on your body, including cancer (Herman, 2012).

Scientists don't know what the "safe dosage" of radiation is. According to Dr. Martin Blank, PhD, a Professor at Columbia University, the human DNA structure is very sensitive to electromagnetic waves. He explains that there are many studies showing us significant potential harm caused by mobiles phones. The Surgical Neurology Journal, in August 2009, published eleven studies with long-term investigation and concluded that those who are heavy mobile phone users and use the device for ten years or more have twice the chance to develop glioma (brain tumour) as compared to those who use it minimally.

So it is wise to avoid long conversations on mobile phones. Don't put them close to your head while you sleep. In addition, those who are more sensitive, such as pregnant women, seniors and children younger than ten years old need to avoid exposure to all forms of radiation.

Cosmetics

Cosmetics are products that you use to clean or enhance your face and body. Although they are good, remember that they may have harmful elements in them, such as aluminium. The danger from cosmetics comes from their chemical content. Some studies have demonstrated more than sixty per cent of chemicals in cosmetics is absorbed and it takes about twenty-six seconds for the cosmetic to enter into your bloodstream (Forster, 2009).

The penetration time and rate are variable; it depends on many factors such as skin type and condition, chemical physical form and category. For instance, the skin on the soles of your feet is very thick, whereas the skin of your eyelids is delicate. Absorption amounts on your face and scalp are five to ten times higher than on other parts of your body (Cal, 2006).

To avoid toxins from cosmetics, it is best not to use artificial products; use homemade or organic skin care products. For example, instead of using a manufactured facial moisturizer, using coconut oil can be a better and safer alternative. In the same way, instead of using regular deodorants, using a rock salt deodorant can help. Look for products that have minimal chemicals and purchase those that are rich in natural ingredients.

In other words, the more fabricated cosmetics you replace with natural products, the less you will be exposed to toxins.

For a complete list with an overview of chemical compounds that you should avoid when buying specific types of products and cosmetics, visit my website at http://www.rswellbeing.com/#!We-Love-to-Smell-great/sma5w/576869dd0cf21d10aa6a0b04 .

PART TWO

THE ACTION PLAN AGAINST STRESS

CHAPTER 5

Taking Out the Trash

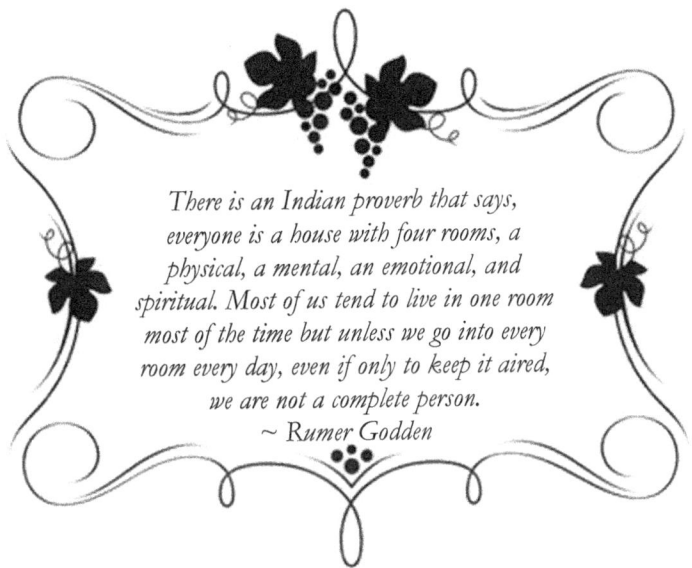

There is an Indian proverb that says, everyone is a house with four rooms, a physical, a mental, an emotional, and spiritual. Most of us tend to live in one room most of the time but unless we go into every room every day, even if only to keep it aired, we are not a complete person.
~ *Rumer Godden*

In the past, if you lived an unhealthy life or were already presenting signs of intoxication or high levels of toxins, you would consider doing a one-day or two-day cleanse. A cleansing time to purify the body has been proven very useful and safe (Morley, 2001).

However, if you are pregnant, detox isn't indicated. In the presence of any medical condition that requires medications (for example, diabetes, cardiovascular disease or any other serious illness), it is in your best interest to discuss the idea of detoxification with your physician or nutritionist first. Because not all physicians endorse fasting, or know enough about it, you'll want to be sure that your health care provider has a sufficient understanding of the benefits of fasting.

It is important that you have a health care provider evaluating your progress to note favourable or adverse effects that detoxification is having on you, especially when you are on a long-term detox program. He or she will monitor your vital signs, such as blood pressure and weight loss. These signs enable your health care provider to make an adjustment in any medication you may be taking. The detox is an excellent way to help the body heal itself. However, it works slowly, because of this, never reduce or stop your medications without your doctor's consent.

As I said in the preceding chapter, toxins can build up in the body, decelerating the system, increasing the acidity and lowering the immune system. This, of course, will increase the risk of degenerative diseases, because of this, the faster you get rid of the toxins in your body, the better. Below you will learn some simple methods that you can use to detoxify your body.

Fibres

Increasing the fibre in your diet is very beneficial to your body. Fibre helps you lose weight and increases your bowel movements, which helps increase the motility of toxins out of your body. It also helps regulate the sugar in your blood. Increase your intake of whole foods, vegetables, salads and fruits, especially plums, bananas, avocados, and papaya, because they have insoluble fibres, which are good for bowel movements. If you have a busy life and aren't consuming fruits as you should be, you can add fibre to your diet through supplements.

Fasting

Fasting for a given period of time, such as three days or more, is another effective method to detoxify the body system. Most religious organizations practice drinking only water for a predetermined time while they are fasting. When you do not eat, your body stores the energy it would have used in digesting the food, because of this, the extra energy is used in healing many parts of your body (Schwalfenberg, 2012).

Fasting is something that you should start gradually; begin with a half day or one full day. With each fast, you can gradually increase the number of fasting days. Fasting is an energy sapping activity; therefore, do not fast when you know that you'll be facing enormous job demands. When you fast, you will get tired, hungry and may get weak. Because of this, it is better to fast while indoors and not walk around the city, especially on sunny days, in an attempt to avoid low blood pressure symptoms.

There are several types of fasting options to choose from, depending on your strength and prior experience with fasting. If you are fasting for the first time, juice fasting may be a good option for you. In this type of fasting, you will feel fewer detox symptoms compared to a water fast. During your fast, you can drink water, vegetable and fruit juice at intervals.

Juice Fast

If you want to drink juice while you are fasting, it is advisable to drink vegetable juice because it has less sugar content than fruit juice. The high concentration of glucose in fruit juice may increase diabetes and candida growth (Page, 1999).

I drink juices that are 60% vegetable and 40% fruit; this gives me a juice with a good taste and reduces the glucose concentration.

Kale, broccoli, celery and cucumbers are among the best vegetables for juicing for the purpose of detoxification because they help keep you nourished during the days you are avoiding solid foods.

A juice fast is the best option for beginners. It will provide you more energy than just water. It is a well-known fact that the first three days of any detox are the most difficult because your body is being introduced to something new. Give your body a little time; it will inevitably adapt by the fourth or fifth day after you commence your detox. However, avoid fasting for more than seven days, and slowly increase solids foods. It is wise to keep having healthy options of foods as soon as you complete your detox.

Water

Drinking plenty of water is another method to wash out the toxins from your body's system. The most healthful types of water to indulge while detoxifying your body is the ionized or alkaline type. Ionized water flushes acidic content from the body. It also has an anti-aging effect and many other valuable properties (Colbert, 2007). Our bodies possess the ability to alkalize themselves; degenerative diseases cannot flourish in an alkaline environment. Moreover, the rate of acidic intake and stress can be too much for the body to counter and reverse. Because of this, you need to help your body increase in alkalinity.

According with Dr Robert Young in his book, *The Ph Miracle: Balance Your Diet, Reclaim Your Health*, most tap and bottled water are low in the alkaline factor; they score around 6.4 to 7 on the pH scale, which is not enough to raise your body's alkalinity. Your blood pH is around 7.3 to 7.5, and any drink you take with pH under the blood pH will make your body expend a lot of energy to balance your body, increasing the alkalinity from the liquid you drank until it achieves the same value of your blood's pH.

It is a good idea to avoid acidic drinks such as alcohol, fizzy drinks, artificial juices, etc, and drink alkaline water instead. There are some water filters where the ionization process occurs naturally using a bio-ceramic filter and natural elements like clay, charcoal, stones, and many other natural materials that can alter the water's magnetic charge. You can also boost the water pH by using an alkaline concentrate known as a pH booster. This has concentrated essential minerals that help increase the pH of the water. It is quick and easy to add when you are ready to drink the water. You can find pH boosters in liquid and tablet forms.

The human heart and brain are comprised of 73% water, the lungs are 83% water, the muscles and kidneys 79%, bones 31% and the skin 64% (Mitchell, 1945). It is obvious that all this water needs constant replacement. It is advisable to drink at least 2 litres of filtered water every day. However, it can vary according to the person's height or weight and health conditions.

Fasting of any kind, whether fruit juice or filtered water fasting, will help you to detox your body and lose weight. The amount of toxins reduces with fat loss as you lose weight.

Detox Shower

Another important method for detoxification is having a detox shower. During a detox shower, you should start with a warm shower and then as your body adjusts, switch to a cold shower. Alternate between the two temperatures for as long as tolerable. This method affects your circulatory system. The warm bath dilates your blood vessels, and the cold bath constricts your blood vessels. After this procedure, you should have improved blood flow throughout your entire body, which will help flush toxins from the system. It has greatly benefited many who continue doing the detox shower.

The detox shower should be done with pure water; make sure there's no chlorine or other contaminants. This can be done using a filter on the showerhead. Detox shower is contraindicated for those suffering from cardiac conditions or serious illness.

Sweating Out

Sweating out toxins is another way to detox. Taking a hot bath or engaging in exercise can help sweat out toxins. Taking a shower after exercising also helps to wash toxins out of the body.

Epsom Salts

Adding Epsom salts to your filtered bath water offers multiple benefits. They are composed from pure mineral compounds of magnesium and sulphate. Because the skin is an extremely porous organ, the body absorbs these minerals. The salts pull out harmful substances like toxins and heavy metals from your cells and help you to de-stress, among other benefits.

It is recommended that you have a detox bath at least once a week. However, to get the full stress-relieving effect, a detox bath is recommended three times a week. A detox bath consists of adding two cups of Epsom salts to the warm filtered water and soaking for about ten to fifteen minutes. Do not use soap or it may interfere with the salts' action. For more benefits, moisturize with olive or coconut oil after your bath. For those who have arthritic joints it is advised to move the joints as much as possible to avoid congestion.

After an Epson salts bath, a good rest is suggested.

Liver Flushes

One controversial, but highly touted, strategy for detoxifying your body is liver flushes. They are considered safe if you are in reasonable health and have no other complicating factors. Before I explain how liver flushes work, I am going to explain the liver's importance in your health.

The liver is a vital organ. The skin is the largest organ in the body; the liver is second largest organ in your body, with numerous functions. The health of your liver is a reflection of you. If your liver is clean and working well, you will be the picture of health. On the other hand, if your liver is not functioning at its full capacity, its ability to manufacture proteins, enzymes, absorb and store vitamins like A, D, E and K, fight infections, detox the body, regulate hormones, regulate sugar and fat metabolism and secrete bile will be compromised.

In addition, an excess of sugars from fructose, carbohydrates and dietary sugar are stored in its tissues, and can result in a condition called non-alcoholic fatty liver, causing sluggishness. Unfortunately, a fatty liver is becoming a common illness today and can be present even in children (Calbom, 2008).

If the liver fails to run well, then you should take action by cleansing it. When your liver is poorly functioning, it works slowly and can lead to significant or permanent damage.

The symptoms of your liver needing some kind of support and/or cleansing are:

- Allergies (Including Skin Itching)
- Puffy and Red Eyes
- Dark Circles Under The Eyes
- Excessive Sweating with Strong Odour
- Psoriasis and Rosacea
- Brown Spots and/or Itchiness on the Skin
- Spider Veins Visible on the Face
- Coated Tongue
- Bad Breath
- Sensitivity to Smells, Especially Chemicals, Petrol Fumes And Smoke
- Poor Immunity (Recurrent Flus, Infections, Inflammations, Chronic Fatigue, Fibromyalgia)
- Diabetes Type 2
- Depression (Persistent Headaches, Mood Issues, Such as Irritability and Anger)
- Intolerance to Fat Foods or Alcohol

- Indigestion and Reflux
- Gall Bladder Stones
- High Cholesterol and Triglycerides
- Poor Concentration
- Atherosclerosis
- Irritable Bowel Syndrome (Constipation)
- Haemorrhoids
- Difficulty Losing Weight
- Lumps of Fat or Cellulite

If you are experiencing any of the above symptoms, it is good to consider phytotherapy and herbs such as milk thistle to support your liver on a daily basis. Milk thistle is the most common herb used to enhance the liver's ability to detox the body. It is taken as a dietary supplement and has antioxidant properties that protect and reinforce the regeneration of cells in your liver.

For deep cleansing and improvement of liver functions, a liver flush protocol is advised. However, if you are recovering from surgery or have a chronic illness, such as cancer or pancreatitis, then a liver/gallstone flush is *NOT* to be done without authorization of your doctor. Please ask your physician before starting the protocol.

If you still have symptoms after a liver flush, it is wise to consider looking for professional advice; some the above symptoms could be linked to other health problems and need better investigation.

Liver Flush Protocol

Before starting the liver/gallstone flush protocol, you should do a seven-day cleanse; this is to make sure the workload on your organs is reduced. Especially in the two days prior to cleansing, you should avoid fatty, fried foods and animal foods (meat, milk, eggs) to prevent overworking your liver. It is

CHAPTER 5: Taking Out the Trash

advisable to do a cleansing prior to the weekend when you can be indoor and able to relax to enhance your quick recovery.

You should adhere to a low-fat diet for about three days prior to commencing the cleanse. Make sure you drink about four cups of homemade apple juice each day throughout the week before the cleansing day. The constituent of apple (malic acid) dissolves gallstones, resulting in improvement of liver functions. If you are diabetic, you can use green apples or ingest malic acid in the form of pills instead of apple juice. In the case of taking malic acid, it is recommended to take that with full stomach (after meals).

Try to avoid all drugs, including medicines, on the day of the cleansing, except for those absolutely necessary, such as insulin or essential pills. Steering clear of drugs will enhance your success with this detox.

Important observation: Do not discontinue your medication except under the supervision of your health care provider.

On the cleansing day, do not eat foods that contain fat, especially from animal sources such as meat, butter, and milk. These high fat foods will put your body into overdrive and increase the workload on the liver. Instead, increase your intake of fruits, natural juices, and cereal for your breakfast and lunch. Lastly, make sure you are able to rest during and the day after your liver flush.

On the cleansing day:

2:00 p.m. - Start fasting (avoiding any solid food after 2:00 p.m.).

8:00 p.m. - Add one tablespoon of Epsom salts (magnesium sulphate) to 200 ml of clear drinking water and drink the solution. You can drink the solution with 1/8 teaspoon of Vitamin C powder or half of a fresh squeezed lemon to improve the taste. You can rinse your mouth with water after.

The Epsom salts work by relaxing bile ducts, allowing the stones to pass more easily. People with Epsom salts sensitivity or intolerance shouldn't do this cleansing protocol.

10:00 p.m. - Repeat by drinking another cup of Epsom salts (one tablespoon of Epsom salts to 200 ml of water).

11:45 p.m. - You should have ¾ cup of citric juice from freshly squeezed lemons and blend it with ¼ of cup of organic extra virgin olive oil. Stir it gently and drink the entire amount while standing up. After this, you should lie in bed as soon as possible. Try to sleep; lie on your back with your head on the pillow or lie on your right side, if possible.

Do not sleep on the left side to avoid any discomfort or pain. The original recipe suggests using olive oil; however, those who feel nauseous when swallowing it can swap it for unrefined coconut oil. The oil is intended to stimulate the gallbladder contraction, helping push out the stones.

8:00 a.m. - Your next dose of Epsom salts and water should be in the morning at 8:00 a.m. when you wake up. You can head back to bed for more sleep after drinking the solution if you want to.

10:00 a.m. - You should take your last dose of Epsom salts and water. If you want to eat after this, you may do so mid-afternoon or two hours after the last dose.

During this process, you will feel the urge to go to the toilet. Grab a light to help you observe and find the gallstones in your stool. You will notice that the gallstones may come in different colours like green, yellow and brown and in a variety of shapes and sizes, and will float while the stool will sink.

The gallbladder and the liver support the digestive system by storing the bile; it is formed from several substances such as cholesterol, bile salts and bilirubin. These substances are secreted into the small intestine when food arrives. However, a poorly functioning gallbladder or liver can form hard particles that turn into stones.

According to English scientific literature, the liver detox is safe, and it has been practiced for thousands of years. Ancient medicine, such as practiced by the Indian Ayurveda and Egyptians, has also described using lime and oil to detoxify the body through the liver. There are some medical registers written in 1920 and 1930 in Germany and England that describe the effects of mixing olive oil and citric juice to dispel stones formed by bile. In these historical registers, officials referred to these stones as intrahepatic gallstones.

Thousands of people have used this protocol and reported no adverse outcomes. I am one of those people. My sons and I have completed liver cleansing with no negative consequences; rather, we found many wonderful benefits, as we practiced it many times. However, I would like to highlight some points from our personal observations completing the protocol.

The protocol requires drinking copious amounts of fluids; however, the intake of Epsom salts increases urination and bowel movements, so it presents a risk of dehydration and the associated side effects. For instance, I had light headache and I felt dizziness during my first cleanse. This is actually very common during the this process of cleanse. The other thing to consider is that Epsom salts are magnesium sulphate, and a large amount of this substance can be toxic and may harm your health. So, don't make the mistake of assuming that increasing the recommended amount of Epsom salts will expedite the process of removing toxins from your body. If you do that, you run the risk of overdose, and can present symptoms such as vomiting, low blood pressure and in the worst scenarios, coma and possibly death. So, be careful!

To optimise your health, the protocol can be done four times a year.

There are many websites on the internet where you can find more information about the liver flush. There is very good content about liver flushing at www.curezone.org. You can also find a more complete protocol from the Dr Hulda Clark at www.drclark.net.

CHAPTER 6

Only the Best for You

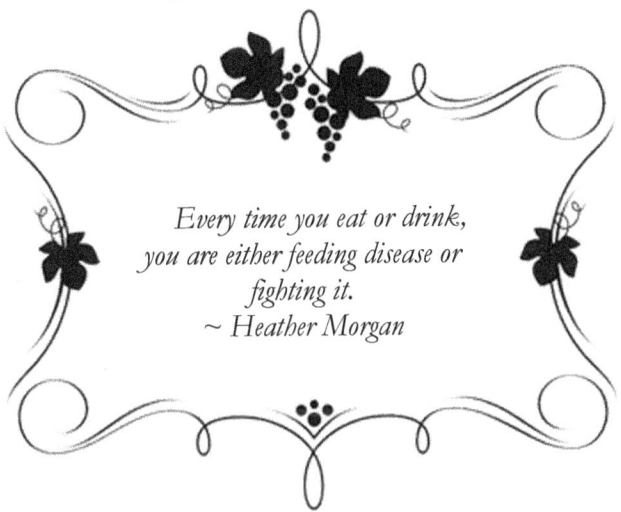

Every time you eat or drink, you are either feeding disease or fighting it.
~ Heather Morgan

Remaining healthy and feeling your best is important at any age. However, it is important you understand that your overall health reflects your habits. If you cultivate good habits, you will have good health. If you don't adhere to a healthy lifestyle, after 30 years, your body will start showing some signals of vulnerability (some people present with this even earlier).

However, if you want to prevent illness or reverse health conditions, improving your overall health and well-being, it is important to consider some changes in your lifestyle starting with your diet. What you eat greatly impacts your physical and, consequently, your emotional health (Nestle, 2002).

Consider that the manner in which foods are produced, grown or raised can affect both your health and the environment. These bring up some questions such as: Are there differences between organic foods and conventionally grown foods? If so, what are they? Which one is the best? Are foods that use biotechnology (research and development) or genetically modified organisms (GMOs) good and safe to consume?

Some research has shown that the use of pesticides, even in small doses, can increase the risk of certain diseases like breast, brain and prostate cancers; Parkinson's; leukaemia and melanoma. Infants and foetuses are most susceptible to pesticide exposure because their fragile immune systems, organs and brains are still developing. If a mother's food consumption consists of large volumes of pesticide-infested foods, she risks passing along pesticides through the placenta and after birth in breast milk, too (Curl, 2002).

Possible consequences of early exposure to pesticides include behavioural disorders, body malformation, motor dysfunction and autism. Some pesticides can cause delayed effects on the brain and nervous system that begin one year after initial exposure.

Many of us have a built-up reservoir of pesticides in our body from years of exposure. Pesticides in the human body can lead to a weakened immune system.

Environmentally, excessive use of pesticides has resulted in the mutation of some vectors of disease (e.g. mosquitoes, flies) surfacing that can only be killed with heavy toxic poisons such as 2,4-dichlorophenoxyacetic acid (the main ingredient in Agent Orange).

The list below shows fruits and vegetables that have been analysed by the Environmental Working Group (EWG). It is a US-based non-profit organization that analyses the results of government pesticide testing of foods produced in the US. According to them, these foods contain the highest average levels of pesticides. Because of their high pesticide levels when grown in a conventional way, it is best to buy these products organic.

CHAPTER 6: Only the Best for You

This foods contain high amounts of pesticides

Apples	Nectarines	Summer Squash
Grapes	Strawberries	Hot Peppers
Peaches	Sweet Bell Peppers	Kale
Celery	Spinach	Cherry Tomatoes
Potatoes	Pears	Green beans
Cucumbers	Tomatoes	

In the UK, according to Pesticide Action Network (PAN UK), flour and bread also contain high levels of pesticide residues.

The list below displays some fruits and vegetables that were found to have the lowest level of pesticides. Some of them have a thicker skin, providing better protection from pests, meaning that they do not need large quantities of pesticides in the growth process.

This foods contain low amounts of pesticides

Papaya	Avocado	Pineapple
Grapefruit	Kiwi	Mango
Sweet Potatoes	Onion	Eggplant
Cabbage	Asparagus	Mushrooms
Sweet Peas (frozen)	Sweet Corn	Cantaloupe

Some products can be washed and it may slightly reduce their pesticide content; however, it is not enough. Peeling the fruit or vegetable may help, but valuable nutrients will come out on the process of peeling of the skin. However, GMOs are most commonly present in US foods such as alfalfa, canola, corn, squash, zucchini, soybeans, wheat and papaya; they also appear in lots of breakfast cereals and processed foods. Pay attention to your favourite canned or packaged meals. If you see names like corn syrup or soy lecithin, there is a huge possibility that it contains GMOs. Because most wheat is modified, gluten has become more prevalent. According to some research, gluten indices in simple bread today have more than 400 times the gluten when compared with our grandmother's bread. It is why so many people are having digestive and reproductive problems. Even if you do not have celiac disease, the bread you are eating today isn't made with the same quality wheat as when you were a child. It is best to reduce consumption of wheat products as much as you can.

Organic Foods

The term *organic* refers to the method used to grow or process agricultural products. You'll often see a dedicated section in a grocery store for organic foods.

Certain requirements must be met to ensure the product labelled as *organic* indeed meets those standards. An organic vegetable, for example, must be grown in nontoxic soil with no artificial alterations and must be clear from conventional products like pesticides.

Farmers are not permitted to use synthetic pesticides in organic farms. In addition, bioengineered genes (e.g. GOs), petroleum-founded fertilizers and sewage sludge-based fertilizers are not allowed (Henneron, 2002). Because of that, organic foods are naturally grown. Some research shows that they may have 300% more beneficial nutrients than non-organic foods, including vitamins, minerals and antioxidants. Furthermore, individuals with allergies to certain foods, chemicals, or preservatives will find their symptoms decreased or stopped in most cases once they begin to consume only organic foods.

There are other beneficial aspects to organic foods:
- Organic products are more perishable, considering they don't have any additives to prolong their shelf

CHAPTER 6: Only the Best for You

life. Generally, they are produced by small local farms. Because of this they are fresher most of the time.

- The organic producing farm is best for the atmosphere. Natural farming helps sustain humanity and protects the environment. It results in less air pollution (air, water, soil), protects water, minimizes soil erosion, increases soil fertility and uses less energy. Farming without pesticides can be a blessing for birds, bees and small animals, as well for those who live near or work on the farms.

- As an alternative to synthetic pesticides or fertilizers, organic farmers nourish the existing soil's components by using water-holding capacity. Organic farms also produce and control pest organisms with biological diversity and compost to make soil amendments to maintain and replace the potency of the soil (Pokharel, 2015).

- Organic dairy products, meat and eggs are produced from animals that are fed organically, non-GMO and they are allowed to roam in open spaces. These animals are housed in positive living conditions that adhere to the natural behaviour of the animals. Ruminants must have access to a pasture. Healthy livestock and chicken do not receive antibiotics, hormones, or medications in the absence of illness; however, they may receive vaccinations to avoid disease. Animal diseases and parasites are controlled primarily with preventive procedures such as hygiene, a balanced diet, rotational grazing and stress control. Organically fed animals may also be 'free-range,' and are given more room to walk around the premises and breathe in fresh and clean air.

The use of antibiotics on animals in conventional farming increases the number of animals harbouring bacteria that is resistant to antibiotics. Because of this, those who consume traditional meat will be less responsive to antibiotics. Conventional farms also feed their animals with by-products, increasing the risk of acquiring mad cow disorder.

GOs and Genetically Engineered (GE)

Organic foods must meet strict criteria to be classified as organic and GMO-free. Both GMO and genetically engineered (GE) refer to crops or animals whose DNA has been artificially altered or combined from crossbreeding (Nestle, 2002). These alterations are intended to increase the foods' resistance to diseases and, in the case of fruits and vegetables, improve their hardiness to be more resistant to insects.

The US Food and Drug Administration (FDA) and biotech corporations producing GMOs claim that they are safe and they are properly evaluated and tested by the FDA before being marketed to consumers. However, many food safety advocates believe that this science is reasonably new. For this reason, there are a limited number of research studies on these foods, and also they have been evaluated for only a very short period (no long-term studies), presenting insufficient data to determine the safety of GMOs in humans and for the environment.

Some research in animals demonstrates that GMOs may destroy organs, impair cognition, and thicken the digestive tract.

It is useful for you to research and to understand what the government of your country permits in conventional agriculture because it varies from country to country. However, in the majority of countries they allow:

- Dairy cows - they agree to the use of antibiotics.
- Beef cows - they have the authorization to use antibiotics. They can use by-products, steroids, hormones, pesticides and sewage sludge.

- Pigs - they agree with the use of antibiotics, sewage sludge, animal by-products, arsenic-based drugs and insect repellent (growth hormones are prohibited).

- Broiler chickens - there is consensus on the use of antibiotics, animal by-products, insect repellent, sewage sludge, arsenic-based drugs (growth hormones are prohibited).

- Egg-laying hens - they tolerate the use of antibiotics, sewage sludge, animal by-products, arsenic-based drugs and insect repellent.

When purchasing products or other foods at the market, pay very close attention to food labels and be wary of potentially deceiving terms.

Natural vs Organic

The understanding of the word *natural* is imperative; it doesn't mean organic. According with the FDA, the term *natural* on food packaging is an unregulated term that can be used by anyone, while organic certification indicates that established standard requirements have been met. More information can be found at

www.fda.gov/aboutfda/transparency/basics.

What is Grass-Fed Meat?

The term 'grass-fed' means that the animals have continuous access to the outdoors, and are fed exclusively on a diet of grass or hay. Livestock are natural ruminants and consume grass, so they tend to be in better health when fed in this way. Furthermore, the beef from grass-fed cows has been shown to contain extra amounts of beneficial omega-3 fatty acids. If the meat is labelled as grass-fed, but not certified as organic, it means the animal was raised on an open pasture, but was exposed to or treated with synthetic pesticides or fertilizers.

What Does Free Range Mean?

The term 'free-range' or 'free-roaming' usually implies that the animals were not restricted to a cage and had access to the outdoors. Unfortunately, there are no specifications about the total time that animals should spend outdoors or the scope of the outdoor space available. The terms free-range or free-roaming do not apply to egg-laying hens. While it is hard to tell what free-range means on meat packaging, the best thing to do is contact the producer and clarify your doubts.

The term cage-free means that egg-laying hens are not raised in a confined space. Nevertheless, it doesn't always mean they have outside exposure.

Why Organic Food Seems to be Expensive

Organic food requires intensive labour to produce, since the farmers do not use any chemical fertilizers, pesticides or drugs. Because of that, organic food production requires many times more hard work than the conventional method.

Obtaining the organic certification and preserving this status is costly. Organic feed for animals can cost twice as much. Organic farms are usually smaller than traditional farms, which means greater overhead costs and bills for a smaller production of produce. Most of these farms are too small to obtain government subsidies; to have their produce sold, they must work as co-op farms.

All the above reasons may be why some organic foods are slightly more costly. Instead of grabbing for the cheaper option at the grocery store, you may want to ask yourself why the alternative is cheaper. Ask, compare and choose what is better for your health. Be wise in your decision!

CHAPTER 7

Building Blocks for the Best Health

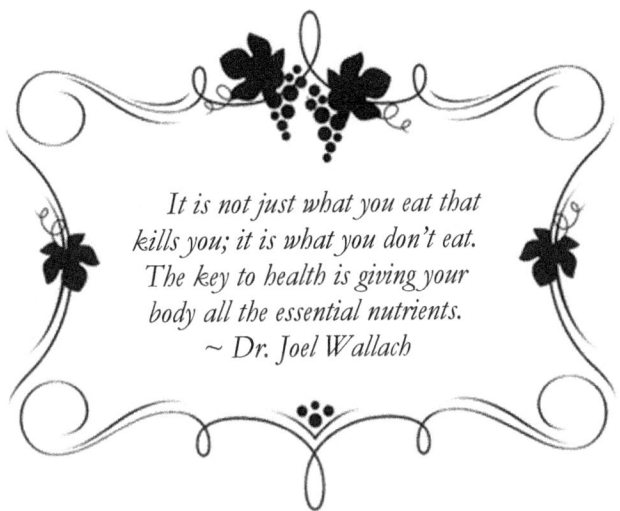

It is not just what you eat that kills you; it is what you don't eat. The key to health is giving your body all the essential nutrients.
~ Dr. Joel Wallach

The human body needs thirteen vitamins for its healthy growth, development and maintenance. They are vitamins A, C, D, E, and complex B vitamins. Vitamins are divided into two categories:

Fat-soluble Vitamins

These are vitamins that are found in the fatty tissues of your body; they are A, D, E and K. Fat-soluble vitamins are best absorbed by your body when consumed with some oil food. Olive oil and coconut oil are good options.

Water-soluble Vitamins

These are vitamins that your body uses immediately; they are complex B vitamins and C. These vitamins are expelled through urine when they are not used right away. The only water-soluble vitamin that is stored in your liver is vitamin B12.

According to many vitamin specialists, *all diseases* occur because of *deficiencies* in one or more vitamins. All the vitamins have specific functions, they are:

Vitamin A

Vitamin A can be derived from animals, it is known as retinol. In fruits and vegetables, it is named as Beta-carotene, which is also known as pro-vitamin A carotenoid.

Vitamin A is essential for preserving eyesight, night time vision, healthy teeth, mucous membranes, skin, sexual reproduction, proper functioning of the organs, formation of tissues, normal growth, development of cells, iron absorption and maintenance of a healthy immune system. It also works in programming growth and development of male and female reproductive organs of the embryo in the uterus.

The carotenoids work as potent antioxidant and anti-inflammatory agents. It has been proven that consuming more natural foods that contain vitamin A, or ingestion in supplement form, can reduce the risk of cardiovascular disease, breast and lung cancer (Omennal, 1996).

A deficiency of vitamin A can cause diseases like exophthalmia, severe acne, psoriasis and retinitis pigmentosa.

Beef and chicken liver are rich sources of vitamin A; you also will find some amounts of vitamin A in egg yolk, butter, cheese, and whole milk.

Beta-carotene is found in carrots, dark green and yellow leafy vegetables like spinach and broccoli, apricots, pumpkin, kale, palm oil, lettuce, goji, mustard greens, Swiss chard, berries, sweet potatoes, butternut squash, broccoli raab, red peppers, tomatoes and cantaloupe.

Night blindness is the primary early symptom you feel as an indicator of vitamin A deficiency. Pregnant women, nursing mothers, infants and children regularly get infections because of deficiency of vitamin A.

The daily recommendation for vitamin A varies by several factors, including age and sex. Recommendations also vary by country. In the UK, men are advised to take 700–1000 micrograms (mcg) Retinol Equivalents (RE) daily. Women should take 600–800 mcg RE per day. In the US, adult men are recommended 900 mcg daily, while women are recommended 700 mcg daily.

Different studies have shown that a large proportion of the world's population does not receive the recommended daily allowance (RDA) for vitamin A from their diets. According to national nutrition surveys, there are small supplies of both the beta-carotene and pro-vitamin A in a large part of the world.

Vitamin B1 (Thiamine)

Vitamin B1 was the first vitamin to be discovered. Vitamin B1 functions as a helper molecule, called a *coenzyme*. Coenzymes activate proteins called enzymes that help your body control biochemical processes. Sufficient amounts of vitamin B1 should be taken because it is essential for converting proteins, carbohydrates and fat in food to energy. It also conducts nerve impulses and helps with the production of nucleic acid in DNA.

The most significant source of vitamin B1 is dried brewer's yeast. However, you can also find it in other sources such as potatoes, spirulina, meat, fish (eel and tuna), milk and whole grains like oats, nuts, wheat, rice, beans, lentils and flaxseed.

It is very rare to find a deficiency in vitamin B1 (thiamine). Most often deficiency of vitamin B1 occurs in people who rely on sugary foods or alcohol for their calories. Difficulty in the digestion of carbohydrates is one primary symptom of deficiency of vitamin B1 (thiamine).

Deficiency of vitamin B1 may cause you to feel fatigue, experience reduced mental alertness, damage the heart, nerves and bones, make breathing difficulty and cause beriberi.

In both the UK and US, the adult recommended dose is 0.9-1.1 mg of thiamine each day for men and women should take 1.1-1.2 mg of thiamine daily.

Vitamin B2 (Riboflavin)

Flavin is derived from the Latin word *flavus*, which refers to the yellow colour of this vitamin. It is among the most distributed water-soluble vitamins in foods. It exists in your body as a coenzyme component. The vitamin B2 helps your body convert carbohydrates to glucose in the production of energy, healthy skin and eyes and in the neutralization of free radicals, which damage cells and DNA.

Vitamin B2 can be derived from milk, dairy products, eggs, lean meat, fish, whole grains, cereals and green leafy vegetables. You also find a high amount of riboflavin in yeast and chicken and beef liver.

In some countries, the recommended daily values of riboflavin range from 1.1 to 1.3 mg for women and 1.3 to 1.6 mg for men.

Those at risk of vitamin B2 deficiency include older adults, those individuals who use high consumption of alcohol, women using birth control pills (these pills diminish the body's ability to absorb this vitamin) and those who do not drink milk.

A deficiency of riboflavin can cause several symptoms, including fatigue, growth deficiency, problems with digestion, lip ulcers and cracks around the mouth, swollen tongue, sore throat and some skin problems.

Vitamin B3 (Niacin amide)

Vitamin B3 is also called niacin amide and is presented in two different forms, nicotinamide and nicotinic acid.

Both forms of B3 form the coenzymes NADP and NAD.

Taking an adequate amount of vitamin B3 (niacin) is essential because it helps your body with several functions such as conversion of food into glucose, production of energy, production of macromolecules like fatty acids and cholesterol and repair of DNA. Several studies have shown that niacin also plays a role in normalizing metabolism, proper functioning of the nervous system, and maintenance of healthy skin and mucous membranes.

You will find niacin in the following foods: meat, fish, milk, yeast, dairy, eggs, seeds, liver, green vegetables, poultry, beans, nuts, lean meats and legumes. The human body has the capacity to transform the amino acid tryptophan when consumed in high doses, into B3.

Vitamin B3 deficiency can result in abdominal upset, weakness, nausea and vomiting, indigestion, loss of appetite, pellagra and depression. Alcoholism is the main cause of vitamin B3 deficiency.

In most countries in Europe and the US, 16 mg NE and 14 mg NE are recommended daily amounts for men and women respectively. About 15-25% of older adults do not meet the recommended amount of vitamin B3.

Vitamin B5 (Pantothenic Acid)

Vitamin B5 derives its name from the Greek word *pantos*, which means 'everywhere', because it is found in all living cells.

A required amount of vitamin B5 is essential, because it helps your body in:

- Converting food into glucose

- Catabolism (breaking down) of fats, proteins and carbohydrates for the production of energy
- Getting rid of bad cholesterol and triglycerides
- Forming red blood cells, sex and stress-related hormones and healthy digestion
- Supporting metabolism, improving mental alertness
- Producing and metabolizing steroid hormones, vitamin D and chemicals that transmit messages in the brain called neurotransmitters
- Reducing fatigue and weakness

The most important sources of vitamin B5 are yeast, organ meats like kidney, liver, heart and brain, eggs, milk, whole grain, cereals, vegetables and legumes.

Deficiency of vitamin B5 is a rare condition and doesn't occur alone, but along with other vitamin B deficiencies. However, alcoholics, women who are taking oral contraceptives, older adults and individuals who have recently undergone surgery can present with vitamin B5 deficiency.

The common symptoms of B5 deficiency are lack of sleep, depression, fatigue, nausea and vomiting, irritability, burning feet, stomach pain and respiratory infection.

Lack of concrete recommended levels of vitamin B5 has led most countries to providing estimates. In some countries, adults take 3 to 12 mg. In 2014, the European Food Safety Authority (EFSA) recommended that every adult, including pregnant women, consume at least 5 mg each day.

Vitamin B6

Vitamin B6 is essential to help with the conversion of glucose to energy, production of neurotransmitters (assists in the transmission of information between nerve cells), hormone production, red blood cells and cells that boost immunity. It also maintains the levels of homocysteine (amino acid that influences heart diseases).

The recommended dosage of pyridoxine varies by age, sex and risk group. The daily dosage ranges from 1.3 to 1.7 mg for men, and 1.1 to 1.5 mg in women.

You can find good sources of vitamin B6 in beef and chicken liver, meat, chicken, veal and pork. Some other good sources include fish like salmon, sardines, tuna, herring and halibut. In addition, corn, whole grain cereals and nuts (walnuts and peanuts).

The symptoms of deficiency of vitamin B6 include confusion, depression and irritability, weakened immune system, skin and mucosa inflammation.

The risk group of vitamin B6 deficiency are the elderly, pregnant women and nursing mothers, women on oral contraceptives, underweight individuals and alcoholics.

Vitamin B7 (Biotin)

Vitamin B7 is also known as vitamin B8 or vitamin H. It is colourless and has about eight forms. D-biotin is one of eight forms and naturally occurs with full vitamin activity.

Your body needs a sufficient amount of vitamin B7 to convert glucose into energy, manufacture fatty acids and amino acids, metabolize normal macronutrients, for normal energy production, normal skin and mucous membrane maintenance, proper functioning of the nervous system, growth and maintenance of the hair and mental health.

The richest sources of vitamin B7 are liver, yeast and kidney. It can also be found in soybeans, egg yolk, cereals and nuts.

Biotin deficiency can be found in people with diabetes mellitus, pregnant women, patients undergoing haemodialysis and patients who are completely on intravenous nutrition.

Symptoms of biotin deficiency are dry scaly skin, hair loss, cracked corners of the mouth, dry eyes, fatigue, and loss of appetite, sleeplessness, painful and swollen tongue and depression.

In Europe, the recommended adult daily dosage of biotin is 26 to 50 mcg for men and women under 65 years old, while the US recommends 25 mcg of biotin daily. The EFSA noted that adults and pregnant women should increase their intake of biotin to 40 mcg each day.

In the UK, national nutrition surveys have reported that most people do not meet the recommendation of the estimated daily intake of vitamin B7.

Vitamin B9 (Folate)

Folate comes from Latin, *folium*, which means leaves. There are different forms of folate that include the naturally occurring folate and folic acid. Folic acid is used in vitamin supplements and is a synthetic compound. Its high level of stability makes it a favourite supplement in fortified foods.

The following highlights the various benefits of vitamin B9:

- Regulates uptake and utilization of amino acids, which are the foundation of protein synthesis
- Production of DNA, the genetic material of the body
- Formation of blood cells in bone marrow
- Ensuring rapid growth of cells in infants, children and pregnant women
- Controlling the level of the amino acid homocysteine
- Formation of blood
- Normal growth of the foetus
- Synthesis of amino acids

CHAPTER 7: Building Blocks for the Best Health

- Normal psychological functions
- Cell division
- Prevention of fatigue and weakness
- Increase of maternal folate level, preventing neural tube defect during pregnancy

Folate sources are dark green leafy vegetables, liver, wheat germ, beans, yeast, milk, beets, egg yolk, dairy products and orange juice.

The most common vitamin deficiency is folate deficiency. It results from inadequate folate intake, abnormal absorption caused by a disorder of the gastrointestinal tract and abnormal metabolism.

Loss of appetite, weakness and irritability are early signs of deficiency of folate. When folate deficiency is severe, it can lead to megaloblastic anaemia, a condition where the bone marrow manufactures large-sized and immature red blood cells.

Those at highest risk of folate deficiency are individuals with alcohol dependency. In addition, pregnant women and nursing mothers are at high risk because during pregnancy a big amount of B9 is required for the baby's tissue growth, and substantial amounts of vitamin B9 are lost through breastfeeding. This is why pregnant women are required to increase the amount of folate/folic acid throughout pregnancy and breastfeeding. Folate deficiency can also lead to neural tube defects.

In the UK, it is recommended for adults to take 200 to 400 mcg of vitamin B9 (folate) every day. In the US, the RDA is 400 mcg for adults, 600 mcg for pregnant women, and 500 micrograms for nursing mothers.

Research shows adults in many countries, including European countries and US, are not meeting the daily recommended dosage of folate.

Vitamin B12

Vitamin B12 is found to be the largest and the most complex among all vitamins. It is made up of molecules containing cobalt. This is the reason why it is called cobalamins. The cobalt gives it a red coloration.

The primary functions of vitamin B12 are:

- Conversion of food into glucose, which gives you energy
- Maintenance of normal healthy nerve cells
- Production of DNA
- Regulation, in conjunction with vitamin B9 (folate)
- Production of red blood cells
- Control of levels of amino acid homocysteine in the blood, in combination with vitamin B9 and vitamin B6
- Support of normal cell division
- Maintenance of immunity
- Proper neurological and psychological functions
- Reduction of weakness and fatigue

Some foods such as liver, kidney, eggs, cheese, milk, yeast extract spreads, whey powder, fish and dairy products are rich sources of vitamin B12.

It is common to find mild deficiencies of vitamin B12 in the elderly and those who had laparoscopic gastric banding (lap-band surgery) to have decreased content of digestive acids, which are needed for the absorption of vitamin B12. In addition, vegetarians usually need an extra supplementation of B12.

Vitamin B12 deficiency can result in some symptoms like difficulty in breathing, anaemia, nervousness, diarrhoea, fatigue and irritability and depression. Neurological damage (brain and central nervous system) can result from severe deficiency.

The daily recommended dosage of vitamin B12 for adults in Europe is 1.4 micrograms (mcg) daily and 2.4 mcg daily in the United States. An additional 0.2 mcg is required for pregnant women and 0.4 mcg for nursing mothers.

Vitamin C

Vitamin C, also called ascorbic acid, is a water-soluble vitamin. Unfortunately, the human body cannot produce vitamin C on its own. We can only get vitamin C from our diet.

Vitamin C is a potent antioxidant with anti-viral, anti-histaminic (anti-allergies) and anti-bacterial properties. Some research shows that vitamin C administered in large doses can fight cancer cells.

Taking adequate doses of vitamin C is essential for you because it helps repair blood vessels and scar tissues and functions in the growth and development of tissues. It also is essential for healing wounds, maintaining the quality of neurotransmitters and preventing damage from free radicals, especially when administered in conjunction with vitamins A, D3 and E.

Vitamin C also reduces the risk for cancer, heart diseases and arthritis. It functions in normal collagen formation, normal function of the bones, cartilage, teeth and gums, blood vessels and skin. It enhances the normal functioning of the immune and nervous system, balances psychological functions and increases non-haem iron absorption. Lastly, vitamin C reduces fatigue and weakness.

Vitamin C can be derived from fruits and vegetables. You will find vitamin C in fruits like guava, strawberries, mango, black currants, citrus fruits (oranges, grapefruits, lemons) peaches, kiwi and lychee. In addition, you can find vitamin C in some vegetable such as broccoli, kale, cauliflower, peppers and Brussels sprouts.

When you are supplementing with vitamin pills, it is preferable you take vitamin C supplements separately, without combining them with other vitamins in the form of multivitamins, for the simple reason that the amount you need does not fit in a multi-vitamin.

Vitamin C in the body can be inadvertently lowered by smoking cigarettes, putting smokers at greater risk of vitamin C deficiency. The signs of vitamin C deficiency include drying and splitting of hair, fatigue, pains in the joints, swelling and bleeding of the gums, rough, scaly and dry skin, inability of wounds to heal on time, bruising easily, epistasis and a decreased immune system. Lower amounts of vitamin C in the body have been implicated in some heart diseases, stroke, hypertension and atherosclerosis. Scurvy results from a severe form of deficiency of vitamin C. This can be corrected by increasing the intake of vitamin C.

The recommended daily dosage of vitamin C is 100 mg in Europe, and 90 mg daily for men and 75 mg daily for women in the US. During pregnancy, most countries require higher doses of vitamin C.

A European nutrition survey found that only 50% of the total population take adequate amounts of vitamin C.

Vitamin D

Vitamin D is made up of a group of fat-soluble compounds and is important in the maintenance of mineral balance in the human body. When vitamin D is synthesized in the body it is called cholecalciferol; it is naturally produced in the skin from exposure to light, through the ultraviolet action (UVB). Vitamin D is a nutrient that does an excellent job of absorbing calcium. It works in conjunction with vitamin A, E, K2, magnesium and boron, helping calcium build and strengthen your teeth and bones.

When used as a supplement, choose vitamin D3 because it is better absorbed by your body. The intake of vitamin D is also important for you, because it helps increase the blood level of calcium and phosphorus. It also works in cell division. Vitamin D supports the immune system and a chronic vitamin D deficiency increases the body's vulnerability to many illness such as cancer, flu, inflammations, depression, osteoporosis and hormonal imbalances.

The valuable resources of vitamin D are fish liver oils and fish from saltwater, such as sardines, herring, tuna, mackerel, and salmon. Meat, eggs, milk, butter and yogurt have scant amounts of vitamin D. People receive the majority of their vitamin D from the sun. However, some factors such as sunscreen, darker skin, and latitude in the north greater than 40 degrees can block or reduce the skin absorption of vitamin D from the sunlight. Because of this, many studies have shown that the global population is deficient in vitamin D, and scientists estimate that over a billion people worldwide have insufficient level of vitamin D.

The absorption of calcium in the body is affected when there is a vitamin D deficiency. When it happens, the body alternatively extracts the calcium from the bone, leaving the bone *weak* (with less calcium) and increasing the risks of osteoporosis and fractures.

Individuals at risk for vitamin D deficiency include children who were exclusively breastfed (because human milk lacks enough vitamin D) and babies of low birth weight. In addition, older adults are more susceptible to vitamin D deficiency because their skin lacks the ability to produce vitamin D and are more likely to have limited mobility and stay indoors away from the sun. Other risk groups include people with liver and kidney impairment who have difficulties absorbing fat, vegetarians, people who are overweight, alcoholics, dark-skinned people, others with limited exposure to the sun and populations that reside very far from the equator. If you are in one of these groups or you are in the wintertime when there is almost zero production of vitamin D by the skin, vitamin D supplements are good alternatives for you to obtain vitamin D.

The Institute of Medicine's Food and Nutrition Board (FNB) in the US developed Dietary Reference Intake (DRI), which established reference values for vitamin D. The recommended values vary by age and gender. Babies from 0-12 months – 400IU; from 1 to 13 years old- 400IU and 600IU for adults, pregnant and lactating women - 600IU; elderly above 70 years old - 800IU. The recommended daily allowance (RDA) for vitamin D established by the FNB refers to the daily amount needed to maintain a normal calcium metabolism in people who are healthy.

The best way to optimize the production of vitamin D is soaking up the sun without sunscreen with at least 40% of the body exposed. The best time is from 10:00 to 14:00 and the ideal sun exposure is until your skin turns slightly red without causing burns (approximately 15- 20 minutes). When possible, it is recommended to take sun at least 5 times a week. Avoid face exposure and always wear a hat because the face has thinner skin than other parts of the body and is easy to age.

Researchers from Harvard University agree that the RDA is low, and they recommend 1,000 IU or 2,000 IU per day. They say some people may need even more, about 3,000 or 4,000 IU per day to maintain adequate vitamin D blood levels, especially those who are facing degenerative diseases.

Vitamin E

Vitamin E consists of a group of eight fat-soluble molecules. Vitamin E is also called alpha-tocopherol. The name originates from the Greek words *toco,* meaning childbirth, and *pherol,* which means 'to bring forth'. The name was used to show that it has a significant role in the reproduction of several animal species. It is a very potent antioxidant, which protects your cells, tissues and organs against the effects of free radicals. It also is important in preventing various health conditions like cancer, heart disease, and body inflammation. It also enhances blood clotting formation to prevent blood loss and regulates how blood vessels are opened and closed.

Vegetables have substantial quantities of vitamin E. Olives, soybeans, corn, palm, safflower and sunflower are good sources of vitamin E. Nuts, whole grains and wheat germ contain more vitamin E. In addition, seeds and green leafy vegetables are very good sources of vitamin E, while fruits, dairy products, meat and fish have low content of vitamin E.

The deficiency of vitamin E occurs to a high extent in those who have problems with fat absorption, liver disease, infants and preterm babies. Some symptoms of deficiency are the loss of muscle mass, muscle weakness, loss of vision, low immunity, nerve and muscle damage and lack of balance in gait. Kidney and liver functions can be damaged due to a significant deficiency of vitamin E. It can also lead to spontaneous abortions and preterm delivery of babies.

The dosage of vitamin E is determined by your age, sex and other criteria. In Europe, the daily recommended dosage for adults ranges from 4 mg to 15 mg alpha-tocopherol for men and 3 mg to 12 mg for women. In the US, the recommended dosage for adults is 15 mg each day.

In European countries, most people take less amount of vitamin E than the recommended dosage. Studies have also shown that about 90% of Americans do not take the daily-required amount of vitamin E.

Vitamin K

This is also a fat-soluble vitamin, which is found naturally in two different forms. Vitamin K1 (Phylloquinone) is present in plants, and the vitamin K2, also known as Menaquinone, is present in dairy products. The primary function of vitamin K is the ability to initiate blood clotting. Vitamin K helps you with bone density and the general health of bones. It also helps in proper cell growth and the functioning of blood vessels.

The sources of vitamin K1 include green leafy vegetables like spinach, endive, kale, broccoli, watercress, Brussels sprouts, lettuce and cabbage. Potatoes, oats, tomatoes, butter, asparagus, vegetable oils and dairy products are other rich sources of vitamin K1.

Vitamin K deficiency contributes to conditions like gastrointestinal disorders, fat absorption issues, Crohn's disease and gallbladder/liver problems. Drugs that can interfere in vitamin K absorption include blood thinning medications and antibiotics. Deficiency of vitamin K also results in excess bleeding, or haemorrhage, from minor cuts or bruising.

The recommended doses vary according to country. Australia, Switzerland and Germany have a recommended intake of 70 mcg each day for men, and women should take a recommended dosage of 60 mcg. The daily recommended dosage of vitamin K for adults in the US is 120 mcg for men and 90 mcg for women each day.

It has been shown that men and women in most countries meet their recommended dosages. An infant should be regularly given vitamin K to prevent deficiency and avoid serious health complications and risks to the child.

Minerals

Your body also needs essential minerals to function properly. There are 60 essential minerals divided into two major groups — the primary (macro) minerals and the trace (micro) minerals. All these minerals are crucial, but the minor minerals are required in small quantities as compared to the primary minerals. An adequate diet has all of the 60 essential minerals.

CHAPTER 7: Building Blocks for the Best Health

The table below displays the principal essential minerals.

Essential Minerals				
Mineral	Major Sources	Major Functions in The Body	Deficiency Symptoms	Daily Required
Calcium(Ca)	dairy products, leafy greens, meats and grains	bone and tooth formation, nerve and muscle functions and blood clotting	growth issue and weak bones	> 200 mg
Phosphorus(P)	meats (specially red), eggs, dairy products and grains	bone and tooth formation, nucleotide synthesis and acid-base balance	weakness, loss of minerals from bone loss	> 200 mg
Sulphur(S)	proteins from many sources	amino acids	impaired growth, swelling, fatigue	> 200 mg
Potassium(K)	meats, dairy products, grains, many fruits and vegetables	acid-base balance, water balance, nerve function	nausea, muscular weakness, paralysis and heart failure	> 200 mg
Chlorine(Cl)	table salts (himalayan pink salt, sea salt, etc.)	nerves, acid-base balance, gastric juice, osmotic balance	muscle cramps, reduced appetite	> 200 mg
Sodium(Na)	table salts (himalayan pink salt, sea salt etc)	acid-base balance, fluids balance, nerve function	muscle cramps, reduced appetite	> 200 mg

Magnesium(Mg)	whole grains, vegetables, leafy greens	responsible for more than 300 functions in the body	nervous system disturbances	> 200 mg
Iron(Fe)	meats (specially red), eggs, vegetables, legumes, leafy greens, whole grains	component of haemoglobin enzyme cofactor electron carriers	anaemia, weakness, impaired immunity	
Fluorine(F)	drinking water and seafood	maintenance of tooth structure	higher frequency of tooth decay	
Iodine(I)	seafood, iodized salts	component of thyroid hormones	goitre (enlarged thyroid gland)	
Others minerals required in trace amounts are Chromium (Cr), Cobalt (Co), Zinc (Zn), Copper (Cu), Manganese (Mn), Selenium (Se) and Molybdenum (Mo). All above minerals are harmful when consumed in excess.				

When mineral levels go down in your body, the incidence of disease goes up! The following table describes how specific combinations of mineral deficiencies are associated with certain chronic conditions or congenital birth defects.

Mineral Deficiency Disease	Congenital Birth Defect
Chromium+Copper+Magnesium+Selenium+Potassium	Heart Condition
Iodine+Selenium+Zinc+Copper	Hypothyroidism
Copper+Iodine+Iron+Magnesium+Zinc+Selenium	Chronic Bronchitis
Magnesium	Asthma

CHAPTER 7: Building Blocks for the Best Health

Mineral Deficiency Disease	Congenital Birth Defect
Magnesium	Insomnia, Anxiety, Abnormal Heart Rhythms, High Blood Pressure Arteriosclerosis,
Calcium+Magnesium+Zinc	Tinnitus
Calcium+Copper+Fluoride+Magnesium	Bone Deformities
Selenium + Vitamin E	Muscular Dystrophy, Steatitis
Selenium	Keshan Disease, Cardiomyopathy
Selenium + EFAs + Copper	Fibromyalgia, Cystic Fibrosis
Copper	Hemorrhoids, Varicose Veins, Aneurysms, Cerebral Palsy, Liver Cirrhosis
Magnesium + Calcium	Osteoporosis, Osteoarthritis
Chromium + Vanadium	Diabetes
Zinc or Folic Acid	Spina Bifida
Zinc + Vitamin A	Cleft Palate, Ventricular Septal Heart Defect

CHAPTER 8

Extra Strengths

Build on your strengths, work on your weaknesses.
~ Minh Tan

As you can see, the food we eat gives us the necessary vitamins and minerals to nourish our bodies or makes us feel sick. Nowadays, there are some problems associated with acquiring such vitamins and minerals from foods. Research shows that because of the increased use of artificial fertilizers and years of neglected soil care, there is a very steep decline in mineral constituents in agricultural soil worldwide. These situations remind us that the foods we eat today are not the same as those of our ancestors. They may have the same appearance, colour and size, but the mineral and vitamin composition has changed drastically.

Unfortunately, as the agricultural land is affected, so too is the quality of the vegetation we consume; it is a vicious cycle. These plants are then fed to animals and people. The decreased nutritional value increases the risk of disease in animals and people. What else can you expect? We are what we eat! There are many studies showing that there is a direct correlation between mineral-depleted soils and illnesses (Grimble, 1994).

Because of this, many doctors and nutritionists recommend extra vitamins and minerals in supplement form to fill voids in the nutritional content of our food. But which supplements can help you? And how do these supplements work in your body?

Multivitamin and Multimineral

A high potency multivitamin and multimineral in supplement form can provide a foundation to keep your body in good health, especially those with a busy routine that cannot eat three to five varieties of fruit a day. A healthy body has the power to perform its natural function of detoxification in a more efficient way, resulting in optimal functioning and weight management. You are responsible for getting the essential nutrients your body needs from the food you consume; however, maybe the food isn't giving us all the nutrients we need to optimise our body functions.

Good multivitamins and multiminerals are relatively easy and cheap to get. Ask your healthcare provider for suggestions on the best brands or check with specialty health foods stores. I highly recommend you choose organic raw supplements or whole food nutritional supplementation. Our bodies are made to recognise and absorb nutrients best when these supplements come from natural and whole foods.

What else do we need aside from multivitamins and multiminerals? Here, I listed other dietary supplements as suggestions that you can choose to incorporate into your diet to maintain optimal health.

Probiotics

Probiotics are essential to reinforce your immune system by helping your gastrointestinal system and improving its

CHAPTER 8: Extra Strengths

absorption of nutrients. It is estimated that nearly 80% of our immune system function is present in the digestive system.

But what is a probiotic? And what does it do in the digestive system?

Probiotics are constituents made up of different bacteria that help restore your intestinal flora. You may be confused. All this time, you thought that bacteria caused disease, so why would you want to introduce these dangerous species into our intestines on purpose?

To understand the importance of probiotics, let's first look at the basic composition of human intestines. Your intestines contain good and bad bacteria. Probiotics (pro = in favour, biotic = life) help maintain an adequate balance. They keep your army of good bacteria alive and in high numbers to battle against dangerous bacteria, helping your intestines to absorb nutrients more efficiently from your food, synthesize vitamins B7, B12 and K and produce other important chemicals that keep you healthy and living longer (Huffnagle, 2008). In addition, the *friendly* flora have the ability to sense the entry of disease, triggering your immune system to kill affected cells. Stress, the use of antibiotics (anti = against/ biotic = life), foods with trace pesticides, highly processed foods, laxative pills, painkillers, antidepressants and malnutrition are the main offenders that can kill good bacteria and impair your immune system.

There are plenty of ways to reintroduce good bacteria into your body quickly. Consume probiotics daily to reconstitute your gut with beneficial bacteria. They will increase your body's absorption of vitamins, strengthen the immune system, promote normal bowel function, and reduce the desire to eat unhealthy food, making your body more nourished and balanced and thus preventing illness.

I recommend that you have at least one daily serving of products such as yogurts, Yakult, kefir, miso, and tempeh because they are examples of foods containing live bacteria, also known as living cultures. Because these bacteria have a short life we need to constantly replace them.

However, you need to keep in mind that bacteria are alive, so they are sensitive to heat, cold and other elements. Therefore, freezing products with living cultures can kill them and fail to produce the probiotic effect they promise.

Alternatively, when it is not possible to consume products with a living culture in food, you may opt for two probiotics in supplement form daily. These tablets contain up to five billion good bacteria.

Kefir is naturally fermented dairy or naturally fermented water. Kefir can have up to 35 billion live organisms in one serving. Because they live longer in your body, they have the power to boost your intestinal flora quickly (Johnson, 2013). It is easier and less expensive for you to culture good flora through your daily dietary consumption than through the purchase of probiotic capsules. Kefir is available in two versions — milk and water kefir, and both have similar health properties.

Fibres

As I said in the Chapter 5, a moderate amount of fibre is recommended in your daily diet. Fibre maintains the diversity and balance of the microorganisms you have in your intestines. Fibres may determine how many calories you can extract and absorb from your food, and aid in limiting the storage of fat.

Proteins

Every organ in your body is made up of proteins. They are essential to the construction and maintenance of organ system, such as muscles, ligaments, tendons, glands, nails and hair just to name some. They not only perform the function of building

CHAPTER 8: Extra Strengths

muscle, they also help in the growth, repair and healing processes of all organs.

The protein consumed from your diet is broken into smaller units called amino acids; they are essential for maintaining your optimal health and vitality. There are twenty-two amino acids, ten of them are called essential amino acids, and the other twelve are non-essential amino acids. The body cannot generate essential amino acids, which means that you must get these from external sources. On the other hand, your body can readily generate non-essential amino acids.

In animal proteins like pork, beef, chicken, eggs, turkey, milk and cheese you find all ten essential amino acids. However, vegetables, legumes, seeds and nuts contain lower levels of amino acids, and may only have one or two types.

The World Health Organisation recommends that men and women get 5% of their daily calories from protein. This means that men should have 38g of protein because they require up to 3,000 calories each day, and women should have 29g of protein because they require 2,300 calories each day.

Low levels of essential amino acids can result in body dysfunction. For example, when there is a deficiency of phenylalanine and histidine, it can result in neurological disorders such as depression. Deficiency of tryptophan can also lead to depression, anxiety and insomnia.

To prevent amino acid deficiency, you should pay attention to what you eat and how you combine it with other foods. If you think you aren't getting enough protein from your diet, you can always use supplementation. The use of amino acids as supplement has helped prevent and treat conditions like mental or nervous disorders, diabetes, epilepsy, chronic fatigue syndrome, heart diseases, herpes and anaemia.

Amino acid supplements can be found in single form or in combination. In supplement form you will find amino acids in

L-form and D-form. In the L-form, amino acids are in their natural form and come from plants and animal tissues. This form is quickly absorbed by the human body. The D-form amino acids are absorbed slowly into the bloodstream and then they are converted to L-form before they are used. Consult your physician before choosing any amino acid supplements. This is to make sure you are going to consume the right quantities and identify which amino acids you need.

THE ESSENTIAL AMINO ACIDS

Arginine

This aids optimal function of the pituitary gland. It promotes and maintains optimal function of the heart and helps in the formation of collagen.

Histidine

This enhances tissue growth. It is important in the maintenance and repair of worn-out tissues. It has anti-inflammatory properties and is vital for children.

Isoleucine

This regulates and maintains blood sugar levels and energy. It also helps in the production of haemoglobin.

Lysine

This enhances the growth and repair of tissues and helps manufacture hormones, antibodies and enzymes.

Threonine

This prevents the build-up of fat cells in the liver and helps in the synthesis of antibodies, which boost the immune system.

Tryptophan

This functions in the synthesis of vitamin B3 (Niacin).

Valine

It has antioxidant action. In addition, it helps break down fats and prevents the accumulation of fats in the liver and arteries.

Phenylalanine

This relieves depression, and can improve mental alertness and memory.

THE NON-ESSENTIAL AMINO ACIDS

Alanine

It boosts the immune system and functions in glucose metabolism. It also improves hypoglycaemia.

Asparagine

It helps balance the central nervous system and synthesise ammonia.

Aspartic Acid

This helps detoxify blood and increases strength and energy.

Cysteine

This helps in detoxification. It enhances collagen production and improves the texture and elasticity of the skin.

Glutamic Acids

This helps maintain brain function and synthesise fats and sugars.

Glutamine

It helps produce glutamic acid for better brain functioning.

Glycine

It helps the central nervous system function, promotes a healthy prostate and helps collagen synthesis.

Hydroxyproline

It is the body's main structural protein and functions in the construction of collagen.

Proline

It helps produce cartilage and collagen. It also works in muscle tissue maintenance.

Serine

This helps in the proper functioning of the central nervous system and the brain.

Taurine

It regulates the excitability of the neurons and the muscles. It gives the brain and heart their optimal production, controlling the heart rhythm, cardiac contraction, blood pressure and platelet aggregation. It acts by increasing the action of insulin, improving glucose tolerance and operating as an antioxidant.

Taurine is essential for the proper function of the minerals calcium, potassium, sodium and magnesium.

It detoxifies liver cells of various toxins. It helps form bile acids and maintains cell membrane stability. Lastly, it reduces the synthesis of lipids and cholesterol that are associated with atherosclerosis.

Tyrosine

It helps to stimulate and modify brain activity and relieves stress.

The Meat Dilemma

In my seminars, many people ask me if they should avoid meat or not. And I teach them - it is up to you. I do eat meat because of the protein content. After I studied this subject, I found that the proteins from vegetables only aren't enough for me. Vitamin B12 is only found in meat, especially red meat. If you opt to avoid meat consumption, it is a good idea to use supplements of at least these three: iron, omega-3 and vitamin B12.

In my view, meat consumption is important. However, because of hormones and animal cruelty, it is best to eat organic meat from animals that have access to pastures. You can see more information about that in Chapter 6. Also, avoid processed meat such as sausages, bacon, salami, smoked ham, chorizo, burgers and hot dogs. According to WHO, all processed, cured, smoked, and salt preserved foods contain chemical substances that highly increase the risk of cancer.

In relation to fish, because of the mercury contamination in the oceans, it is best to consume fish that come from deep cold waters, such as tuna, sardines, and salmon. Pay attention to where the fish come from because fish that are farmed, especially salmon, are full of contamination and don't offer the benefit of omega-3.

It is good to remember that meat increases the body's acidity; if you are eating meat constantly, it is a good idea to have at least one day of detox per week.

Essential Fatty Acids

Essential fatty acids are fatty acids that cannot be manufactured by the body and must be obtained through foods. The groups of essential fatty acids are omega-3 and omega-6 fatty acids, also known as polyunsaturated fatty acids (PUFA). Most of the PUFAs are derived from plants and fatty fish.

Omega-3

Fatty acids are found in three forms. These include alpha-linolenic acid (ALA), eicosapentaenoic acids (EPA) and docosahexaenoic acids (DHA). The ALA usually is converted in the body into EPA and DHA. This conversion is typically to supply the levels needed in the body.

The European Food Safety Authority (EFSA) has explained that the intake of PUFA, DHA and EPA afford significant benefits to human health. The EFSA provides policy makers with scientific advice. They state that these essential fatty acids help maintain a healthy blood pressure level and normal blood levels of triglyceride. It also helps in the proper development and maintenance of brain function, enhances sight and boosts immunity.

Fatty fish like tuna, salmon, sardines and anchovies contain omega-3 fatty acids. Algae and krill are other marine life rich in omega-3 fatty acids. ALAs are also found in nut oils.

The following are sources of omega-6 fatty acids: soybeans, corn oil, sunflower, seeds, nuts, corn, poultry, eggs and meat.

Omega-3 fatty acids and omega-6 fatty acids can also be consumed as dietary supplements.

Individuals with conditions that cause poor absorption of fat may develop a deficit of essential fatty acids. For instance, deficits may be developed by those with conditions such as cystic fibrosis, eye conditions or persons receiving nutrients intravenously.

Deficiency of essential fatty acids also can result in skin conditions, poor circulation, mental health problems and poor memory.

It is crucial to keep a balance of omega-3 fatty acids and omega-6 acids in your food intake. This is because they both work together to promote optimal health. Omega-3 fatty acids help reduce inflammation. However, omega-6 fatty acids promote inflammation. When there is an imbalance in omega-3 fatty acids and omega-6 fatty acids, you are liable to develop disease.

Your diet should have about two to four times more omega-6 fatty acids than omega-3 fatty acids to maintain health. Unfortunately, in developed countries, diets contain fourteen to twenty-five times as much omega-6 fatty acids than omega-3 fatty acids (Simopoulos, 1999). Researchers believe that the rise of inflammatory disease is caused by the imbalance of essential fatty acids. Inflammation is a common precursor to many serious illnesses such as heart disease (Welch, 2010).

There is a consensus between EFSA (European Food Safety Authority) and USDA (US Department of Agriculture) about the suggested intake amount. They suggest 250 mg of EPA/DHA daily for adults and 300 mg of EPA/DHA daily for pregnant and lactating woman.

CHAPTER 9

Right to Dream

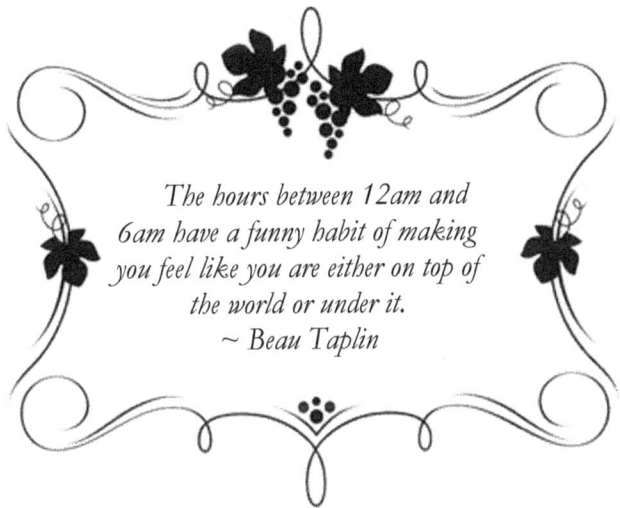

The hours between 12am and 6am have a funny habit of making you feel like you are either on top of the world or under it.
~ Beau Taplin

Your rest time is as important as your work time or the time you expend with your family and friends, but many people don't realise that. However, the quality of your sleep impacts your mental and physical health. Do you know how much sleep is necessary? Restful sleep greatly increase your stress tolerance.

The National Institutes of Health (NIH) says that an adult should sleep for an average of not less than seven hours each night. Sleeping around seven to nine hours is crucial for normal functioning. Hormone, muscle and cell reparations occur during this time. If you have micro-awakenings during the night, your body cannot recover properly and over time your health starts showing signals of sleep deprivation.

Do you feel that after a night of sleep you are still groggy during the day? If so, and if it happens constantly, it may be indicative of something more going on.

It is important for you to understand that sleep deprivation is frequently the result of unrecognised sleep disorders. It is often linked to a physical or mental health condition. Maybe you justify your poor sleep pattern as simply stress from work or worries about your children, or you might think that since you have always slept only few hours, sleeping a few hours a day is perfectly normal.

Many people are unaware that they suffer from sleep disturbance. Lack of information and investigation makes sleep disorders a long-term condition.

Insomnia is a term used to describe a person's inability to fall or stay asleep (Roth, 2007). Generally, those who experience insomnia suffer from low energy, irritability, fatigue, mood disorders, and memory problems.

There are two types of insomnia: acute and chronic insomnia. Acute insomnia occurs for a short duration, such as during a worrisome episode after receiving bad news or due to anxiety, such as when preparing to travel and needing to wake up very early for fear of missing a flight. With acute insomnia, your sleep may be disrupted for one or two nights, but requires no treatment. Usually, you return to your usual sleep routine relatively fast.

In chronic insomnia, the sleep disturbance takes longer to be resolved and usually requires some kind of treatment to recover healthy sleep patterns. Possible causes of chronic insomnia can be physical or mental disorders, side effect of certain medications, or unhealthy habits, such as too much caffeine, cigarettes, use of screens at bedtime (mobile phone, TV, computers) and constant changes in bedtime.

The amount of sleep required is not the same for everyone. Some studies show that there are difference between women and men. Usually, women need more hours of sleep than men do and 40% more women than men report insomnia (Lamberg, 2007). Most healthy adults need seven to nine hours of sleep every night. Children need even more than that. Some still believe that as we get older, our need for sleep decreases. In fact, older adults continue to require about seven to eight hours. Sleeping more or less than that amount may be associated with other chronic health conditions. If older adults have difficulty sleeping well at night, taking naps throughout the day may be a wonderful idea. It will help them recover from the loss of sleep at night.

To evaluate whether you're getting the right amount of sleep, assess how you feel during the day and document the hours you slept the night before. You'll begin to see a pattern. When you have enough sleep, you'll feel rejuvenated, energized, and alert during the whole day.

The amount of sleep you may get and the amount you really need differ. The amount of sleep you need is what will make you function optimally. If you spend more than your usual seven to eight hours in bed, it will improve your brain's performance and cognitive processing. Researchers at the University of California, San Francisco, discovered a gene present in some people that cause them to sleep for a mere six hours at night and still function optimally during the day. However, this gene is very rare. It exists in just 3% of the population.

The most important regulator of sleep is our brain's internal clock, which is affected by light and darkness and is known as the circadian rhythm. In response to the loss of daylight, your body produces melatonin. This hormone makes you sleepy. During the daytime, melatonin production is inhibited by sunlight, which keeps us awake. Your circadian rhythm may be affected by night shift work, travelling across different time zones or sleeping patterns that are irregular. The production of melatonin can be influenced by the lack of sunlight during the day and use of powerful lights at night or the use of screens like iPad, mobile, computer and TV before bed.

Some people may think that after night shift work, they can have the same quality of sleep they would have slept at night by making up the equivalent hours. This is not true. Sleeping during the day cannot equate to the quality of sleep at night. This is why the sleep cycle is complicated.

At night, sleep cycles through a pattern, moving between stage one (deep restorative sleep), stage two (alert stage), and stage three (dreaming rapid eye movement, or REM, sleep). Sleep alternates between REM and the non-REM stage about every ninety minutes. This exchange occurs about four to six times through the night (Ribeiro, 2004).

People move through various stages of sleep as the night progresses. For instance, deep sleep happens in the first half of the night. Later on, your REM sleep becomes longer, alternating with the light stage of sleep. It explains why you are more susceptible to waking up in the early morning, not soon after going to bed.

You may think that it is only the number of hours you spend in bed that matters. The quality of sleep during those hours matters, too. If you find it difficult to stay alert during the day and you think you have spent quality time at night sleeping, it means you have not completed your necessary quality time in each stage of sleep.

There are different benefits derived from each stage of sleep. Stage 3 is where deep sleep and REM occur and is crucial. It is okay to complete 50% of the total sleep time in stage 2, 20% in REM sleep, and 30% in stage 1.

Depriving yourself of deep sleep is harmful to your health. During the deep sleep stage, the body repairs tissues and builds up enough energy to function during the day. This stage maintains your health and initiates the growth and development of cells. This is the stage during which your tissues and muscles are repaired and your immune system is strengthened. When you get a high quality night's sleep, you will wake up feeling refreshed and energised.

Several factors can negatively influence the quality of deep sleep. They are:

- Outside noise (for instance, when a baby is crying)
- Night shift work, since getting good sleep during the daytime is always difficult due to outside noises
- Substances such as nicotine, caffeine and alcohol (Reduce your intake to avoid lack of deep sleep.)
- Being overweight (can cause sleep apnoea)
- Overactive bladder (can make the sleeper wake up many times during the night with the urge to urinate)
- Side effect of some medications such as antidepressants, steroids, and some medications to combat chemotherapy side effects

Chronic sleep deprivation has a harmful effect on your body. It can interfere with your safety, health, performance and alertness. In addition, it decreases your ability to cope with stress, causes memory and cognitive impairment, reduces your level of immunity, and increases your susceptibility to colds, allergies and infection. It also affects weight management, increases the risk for heart diseases and diabetes, and many other health issues. Furthermore, poor sleep quality hinders your ability to make decisions, can lead to depression and irritability and decreases your creative ability while making it harder to solve problems, causes mental fatigue, general malaise, and reduces your motivation.

Because poor sleep decreases motor skills and cognitive functioning, it doubles risk of occupational accidents. According to the National Highway Traffic Safety Administration (NHTSA), every year in the US, driver fatigue is responsible for roughly 100,000 automobile crashes, 71,000 injuries and 1,550 fatalities.

While it is challenging to control things that make you worry throughout the day, you can learn different approaches for responding to sources of stress and worry by managing your mind. This, in turn, will help you to sleep better at night.

Your mental health is as important as your dental or physical health. If you spend five minutes three times a day brushing your teeth, why not take five minutes three times a day to calm down? It is quick and effective to care for your mental health. Weekend lazy time and holidays also *must* become part of your schedule as stress management promotes good health.

In addition, having help in stress management is a good idea, when you're in challenging situations or stressed over work, family and school. Do not let stress affect your day-to-day activities and sleep at night. Always have a positive outlook and try to 'chill out' during the day to sleep better at night.

Relaxation

Relaxation brings innumerable benefits to individuals with sleep problems. Learning how to relax can do wonders for you. It enables you to calm down and get ready for a deep sleep.

Some techniques for relaxation are:

- Deep breathing - When doing deep breathing, you should close your eyes and take deep slow breaths; it works better when you are in contact with nature.
- Muscle relaxation - Release all your muscles from your toes to your head.

- Visualization - You should imagine a beautiful place or an activity that is very good and peaceful. Remain focused on how calm the place makes you feel.

Exercises

Regular exercise is another good way to promote a good night's sleep. Any combination of twenty to thirty minutes of activity during the day can vastly improve the quality of your sleep. Other suggestions to increase physical activities are dancing, gardening or going for a bicycle ride.

You can decide to exercise in the morning, in the afternoon, or at the beginning of the evening. Exercising is very important even in the evening because it increases your temperature. If you dislike vigorous exercise, you can try relaxing options like yoga, Pilates, tai chi or gentle stretching.

Herbal Remedies

Many insomnia sufferers turn to herbal remedies as a first option of treatment. There are some remedies, such as lemon balm or chamomile tea, that are not harmful; but others can have serious side effects and interfere with prescription drugs. St. John's Wort, for example, can limit the efficiency of some drugs, such as contraceptives, blood thinners and some cancer medications. Seek the advice of a health care professional or sleep specialist if you are using medical prescriptions before opting for an herbal remedy.

For those not taking pharmacological medicines, several herbs can help you sleep. For example, valerian root, kava kava, passionflower and lavender are known as stress relievers and can be found in supplement form or tea. It is recommended that they be taken one hour before bedtime.

Melatonin

As mentioned before, the production of melatonin occurs at night. Darkness triggers an increased production of melatonin and its level remains high throughout the night.

It is important to pay attention to the constituent of products that influence the production of melatonin. About 1.3 grams of melatonin will increase its level to up to 20 times what is present in the body and will make you fall asleep. Research shows that the body best absorbs melatonin as a supplement in a sublingual form.

Tryptophan

Tryptophan is a protein that converts into serotonin in the brain, which helps you sleep.

Some people feel that eating a light snack before bedtime can enhance sleep, and it is true. Taking a cup of milk or crackers with cheese before bed will enhance tryptophan's ability to cross the blood-brain barrier and make you sleep easier. Nuts, seeds, soups and sauces also function in the same way.

L-tryptophan is a tryptophan supplement form and, according to some research, it has been proven to have properties that helps people fall asleep when consumed one hour before bedtime.

If you have sleep problems, this may help you. Try a combination of tryptophan (500 mg), L-thiamine (400 mg) and magnesium (500 mg) together instead of the conventional sleeping pills. This combination has helped people to sleep deeply naturally without feeling drowsy the next day. It is effective for acute insomnia and some cases of chronic insomnia, too. However, some more complicated chronic insomnia won't respond to that. In this case, visit your doctor. You will probably need other interventions, such as CBT and/or prescribed sleeping pills for a short time as treatment.

Eliminate Obstructions to Sleep

To improve your sleep, it is important to pay attention to other aspects that can be potential barriers to falling and staying asleep.

Investigations show that one of the best methods to treat insomnia is by changing your sleep environment and behaviours at bedtime. Even if you have decided to use medications for a short time, specialists recommend that environmental and behavioural changes are best for a long-term solution to insomnia. The study's results says that some changes are more effective than prescription drugs; they offer few to no side effects or risk for dependence and they are free!

Here are some suggestions:

- Change bright light bulbs. Avoid the use of intense bright lights at night. They prevent you from sleeping because they inhibit the production of melatonin.

- Always turn off computers and televisions. The light from the television and computers prevents melatonin production. Television does not make you relax. Listening to music or audio books is a better option for relaxation. It is better to record your favourite night-time TV shows. This way, you can have a better night and rest for longer.

- Avoid reading using tablets after 6:00 pm. Reading from a backlit device at night (e.g. tablets such iPad, Kindle, and mobile phones) can affect sleep. It is better to use an e-Reader or paperback for reading your books rather than other electronic devices.

- Darken the room. The darker the room, the more melatonin your body produces. Cover windows with heavy curtains to prevent light from coming though.

- Use red flashlights to navigate your way to the bathroom. If you wake up at night to use the bathroom, use a red flashlight to avoid disturbing melatonin production.

- Balance your fluid intake. Avoid drinking a significant amount of fluids before bedtime to prevent frequent waking up.

- Avoid caffeine, cigarettes and other stimulants after 6:00 pm.

Overactive Bladder

Typical symptoms include urinating more than eight times per day (urinary frequency) and a strong, sudden desire to urinate (urinary urgency) (Van Kerrebroek et al., 2002).

About 33 million adult Americans age eighteen years and older have an overactive bladder (OAB) and may wet the bed (Stewart et al., 2003). The typical symptoms consist of frequent urination (more than 8 times a day) and strong urge to urinate, especially at night. Sometimes the urge results in wetting the bed. Even if they wake up and go to the bathroom in time, this makes them wake up frequently to urinate, preventing them from getting a good and restful night's sleep. If you are in this situation, it is a good idea to visit your doctor.

There are many effective interventions to help you alleviate this, such as conventional medication, herbs, behavioural changes, pelvic floor exercises, and bladder training. Cortisol hormone imbalance also can cause frequency in urinating. Oestrogen imbalance in the case of women and testosterone imbalance in the case of men can trouble the sleep routine, especially during menopause/andropause period. It is good to ask your doctor to test your hormone levels. After checking your hormones, if the imbalance is the case, your doctor will advise you on the best course of treatment. However, if hormone modulation therapy is recommended, you may still consider the natural approach to avoid many side effects of synthetic pills.

There are a number of supplements that "mimic" our natural hormones. Proper hormone modulation using natural hormone replacement therapy can relieve symptoms and prevent degenerative diseases, improving physical and mental functioning.

Some Final Comments About Sleep

If you tried and nothing seems to work on improving your sleep and your doctor determines that you will benefit from a sleeping pill, make sure that you understand how it works. Most times, sleeping pills only work effectively short-term. Sometimes medications and sleep aids complement a behavioural treatment for sleeplessness when the lack of sleep is severe.

Avoid taking sleeping pills for a long time to prevent tolerance and dependence. It is better to keep updating your doctor so your doctor will be able to monitor possible side effects.

Remember that sleeping pills cannot solve your sleep problems instantly and it doesn't cure the cause of insomnia, but rather it can mask the problem and make it worse.

You also can use technology to help you with your sleep problems. An app called Sleepio can give you some extra help. It has a free test to check how good your sleep is and also some advice for treatments based on CBT (Cognitive behaviour Therapy). CBT is proven to be an effective therapy to help people overcome insomnia (Espie, 2010).

For more information at www.sleepio.com.

CHAPTER 10

Exercise: The Easy Pill for Happiness

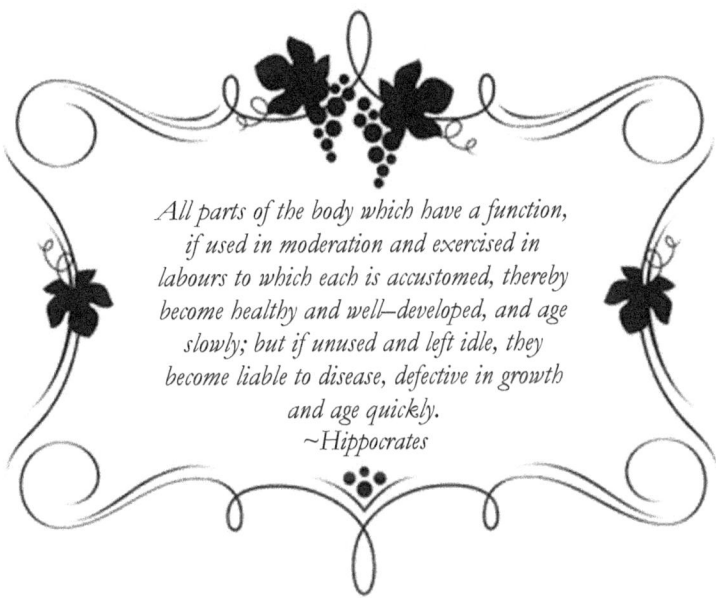

All parts of the body which have a function, if used in moderation and exercised in labours to which each is accustomed, thereby become healthy and well-developed, and age slowly; but if unused and left idle, they become liable to disease, defective in growth and age quickly.
~Hippocrates

We now live in a hyperactive society. Pollution, sedentary lifestyles, and unhealthy diet habits have become part of many people's routines, making it even harder to control the swiftness of the aging process and stay disease-free. However, being disease-free isn't enough anymore. According to the World Health Organization (WHO), the concept of being healthy goes beyond this. It means being fully energized, living well and enjoying life.

Any person who isn't living and feeling "plenty of life" in all aspects - physical, emotional and social - isn't considered healthy, but sick. Fortunately, the number of people becoming aware of the necessity to make lifestyle changes to optimize their overall health is increasing. The number of people adhering to exercise programs is also growing. They are aware of the many benefits exercise brings to the body, including sharp memory, good shape and toned body.

The NHS and American Heart Association suggest at least twenty to thirty minutes of aerobic exercise per day. There are many approaches for beginning an exercise routine, from the easier and simple workout, like reaching the traditional 10,000 steps a day, to a more intensive workout using weights. If you never engage in any exercise, or if it's been a long time, it is good to start with an easy routine. Depending on how your body responds, increase the number of exercises or intensity of your routine. You only need minimal practice to keep your physical and mental health in good shape.

Exercise for Mental Health

There's more to exercise than you might guess. It's not only about building muscles and toning your body. Exercise can bring about major improvements to your mental health. So if you're dealing with tension, stress, anxiety, attention deficit hyperactivity disorder, insomnia or depression, engage in a routine of exercises and enjoy the benefits it will bring to you.

No matter your age or fitness level, when practiced on a daily basis, you'll notice that exercise is a great stress reliever and a powerful tool to make you feel better.

Aerobic exercise can provide you with the following set of benefits:

- **Increased flow of energy** - After working out, your energy levels will spike, helping you to complete your daily tasks easily

- **Greater relaxation** - If you feel tense throughout the day, a workout session will calm you and bring you peace of mind.

CHAPTER 10: Exercise: The Easy Pill for Happiness

- **Better sleep** - As mentioned in the previous chapter, if you're experiencing insomnia, regular exercise will help you relax and get a better night's sleep.

- **Better memory** - Exercise increases blood flow and oxygen to all the organs. Numerous studies have shown the positive effects of exercise on memory; some of them include better thinking skills, less brain fog and sharper memory.

- **Better self-esteem** - Exercise is a powerful way to increase the detoxification of your body by eliminating toxins through sweating and burning up fat tissues. Exercise is closely connected with your emotions by improving your self-esteem and levels of self-confidence.

- **Improved sex life** - As mentioned, physical activity increases your energy levels and hormones and both work wonders at increasing libido, too.

- **Greater longevity** - Exercise reduces the risk for diabetes, heart problems, stroke, high blood pressure and aids in weight loss; these benefits contribute to and even add more years to your life.

- **More positive attitude and outlook on life** - Exercise encourages the production and release of many hormones, helping to balance out your hormones. It stimulates the release of endorphins into your body, known as *happy hormones* and decreases cortisol, also known as the *stress hormone*.

When practiced regularly, exercise works as a natural anti-depressive and anxiety alleviator.

Let's take a closer look at how exercise works as an anti-depressive fighting against depression, anxiety and stress.

How Does Exercise Actually Fight Depression?

Numerous studies have shown the positive impact that exercise has on fighting depression. If you're coping with mild to moderate depression and want a natural and effective solution to eradicate depression once and for all, consider incorporating more exercise into your daily routine. It will definitely improve your mental health and you will start feeling the benefits in around two weeks.

In comparison to antidepressants, exercise promotes the release of endorphins into your body, therefore improving your mood and increasing the flow of energy. Subsequently, exercise produces changes within your brain that promote neural development and minimize inflammation.

In the majority of cases, exercise can also help you escape from negative thoughts and emotions and can prevent the relapse of depression. This is why a large number of people fighting depression have claimed to have achieved fast results by incorporating more exercise into their lives.

Exercise: The Anxiety Fighter

Anxiety is a very unpleasant condition. Experiencing constant worries and fears can make you feel exhausted and have other negative implications in your physical and mental health. When you engage in any kind of activity, you make your body move more. As a result, your body releases those beneficial hormones that I mentioned earlier. In addition, exercise helps you focus on your body's sensations during the time you are performing the activity instead of focusing on your worries and fears; it works like a meditation called mindfulness.

While engaging in outdoor activities like biking, climbing, running or walking, you will experience even more benefits such as feeling the sensation of the wind and/or the sun on your skin, experiencing the sound of birds singing, etc.

CHAPTER 10: Exercise: The Easy Pill for Happiness

It doesn't matter what kind of anxiety you have, be it mild, moderate or severe. You will still reap huge benefits by incorporating a regular workout routine into your life.

Moving to Fight Stress

Stress is reported by more than 75% of the worldwide population. The hectic modern lifestyle is a main reason behind this alarming number. Stress isn't an illness by itself; however, in high levels and on a constant basis, it is a serious condition that must be treated. If not, the chaotic routine will feed the stress, which will eventually result in a huge physical and emotional collapse. Therefore, if you want to avoid an emotional collapse, you must take responsibility and rein in your stress. The easiest and most efficient way to control stress is to work out on a daily basis. It doesn't really matter what kind of exercise you prefer to do. It might be an aerobic activity, such as cardio or jogging, or you might prefer to engage in sports, such as swimming, tennis or badminton. The most important thing is to start moving more. It will eventually clear your mind, relax your muscles and alleviate your tension.

Swimming is an incredible form of exercise; however, be aware of the chlorine content in the water. High levels of chlorine in the water can be dangerous because it is rapidly absorbed by your skin and enters your bloodstream. Iodine, the key mineral that feeds your thyroid, is sensitive to chlorine in the water, meaning that when chlorine enters your body, iodine comes out. Many regular swimmers develop serious conditions associated with thyroid dysfunction due to iodine deficiency from high chlorine content in the water. To avoid overexposure, the best thing to do is avoid swimming pools that use chlorine to treat the water and opt for one that uses ozone as the form of water treatment. However, if you are a regular swimmer, consider having your iodine levels tested. If they appear to be low, it may be a good idea to take medical advice and increase the intake of iodine in supplement form to maintain your health.

Now that you know all about the effects of exercise on your emotional health, you might think that you're ready to go and embark on this journey of rehabilitation and recovery. But that's not all. There are still plenty of things you should know in order to ensure you choose a safe way to improve your health. When it comes to exercise, you must stay within safe levels to avoid injury or inadvertently worsening your condition.

How Much Exercise Is Enough?

You might think that a little bit of exercise is enough to improve your health. Well, it doesn't really work like that. Of course, five minutes of exercise is better than nothing and it can boost your energy levels, providing you with a clear mind or even relax your muscles. But, it's not enough to start alleviating conditions like depression and anxiety. Therefore, a twenty-minute walk around the neighborhood is beneficial, but not enough to begin seeing major positive results. In this case, you'd have to intensify your workouts whilst taking into consideration any limitations on your health. If you deal with severe anxiety and you get strong palpitations every so often, you will have to avoid intense workouts to avoid straining your cardiovascular system. In the case of depression, if an intense workout makes you feel good, then you should definitely continue with them.

As mentioned before, in order to keep your heart in good shape and your body toned, health care practitioners and researchers recommend a minimum of fifteen to thirty minutes of aerobic activity five days a week. And it doesn't really matter whether you decide to invest in a gym membership or do the entire workout at home. Nowadays, there are plenty of videos and TV programs you can watch at home. Many of them demonstrate various routines without the need for any fancy or expensive equipment. The best exercises are those that engage both your legs and arms at the same time, such as walking, dancing, running, swimming, climbing and more.

Moderate aerobic activity is highly recommended to achieve optimum health. Make sure that you stick to such a regimen if you really want to see improvement in your mental health and boost the quality of your life. If you're new to exercise or you have been living a sedentary lifestyle for a while now, make sure that you start with mild exercises for as little as ten to fifteen minutes in order to get your body ready for more intense workouts. For anxiety, make sure that you start every workout session with a deep breathing technique to ensure the flow of oxygen and relaxation within your body.

When is the Best Time to Exercise?

You need to pay attention to your energy levels during the day and schedule your workout session around your peak energy period. You want to exercise when you're most energized so as to not only have fun but also improve your mental health condition. Some people like to exercise in the morning before going to work as a way to energize their bodies and boost their productivity throughout the day. Some like to work out at lunch or during the day. It really doesn't make any difference when you exercise. The most important thing is that you do it and do it on a regular basis!

Practical Tips to Keep Your Focus When Depressed or Anxious

When something is weighing you down and you feel fatigued and depleted of energy, you will have to start your workout session slowly.

A "pre-workout" routine, such as walking your dog, going to a store to buy some food, going out for a walk, etc., can all be of help. Anything that can make you get out of your bed and into the world works for this purpose.

More tips:

- Invite a friend to exercise with you. Working out in a group seems to be a great idea for those who suffer from depression or anxiety. It is a great way to avoid zoning out and to socialize. Distraction from the norm will help you focus on exercise rather than on your problems.

- Don't forget to reward yourself after each workout session as a way to boost your desire to work out next time. A nice reward may be as simple as watching your favorite TV program or movie or enjoying a relaxing bath after a workout.

What if You are Not in the *Mood* to Work Out?

We are human and sometimes we feel tired or too lazy to work out. Instead of forcing yourself into doing your regular workout, you can skip it and engage in one of the following exercise alternatives:

- Engage in vigorous home cleaning. Home cleaning can be a great alternative to your regular workout session. You're going to kill two birds with one stone – get your house clean and get your mind and body in order.

- Use the stairs instead of the lift (elevator) at work or home. You really want to maximize the number of movements you do during the day. So, a good way to get it done is to say no to the lift and use the stairs instead.

- Listen to your favorite music and dance your heart out. I love it and I personally use this. It not only serves as a cheap and fun workout session but as a great method for stress relief.

CHAPTER 10: Exercise: The Easy Pill for Happiness

- Invite your friends over for a social game. Social games today are widely cherished because they help you interact more and optimize your life for positivity and peace of mind. So call your best friend and tell her or him to run over to your place with the yoga mat.

- Explore your city in the evening. Some people live their entire life in the same neighborhood, but never get the chance to know the city in which they live. This is the perfect opportunity to change this. Take your GPS with you or use Google Maps from your mobile phone and roam the streets in the evening. This will not only serve as a great workout but also a good way to relax your mind and body as well as boost your mood.

- Park away from your house or work. So if you're commuting by car during the day, consider parking your car 100 meters away from your house or office to force yourself to walk to your destination by foot.

- Go through your clothes and throw away or donate anything you don't wear anymore. In feng shui, when you get rid of the old, you get rid of your problems and start a new life. So why not use this tip to do both? Improve your mental health and perform a moderate exercise. Walking to the places to donate your things is a good way to exercise your body and your compassion for others.

Now that you are armed with tools and information on how exercise can positively improve your physical and mental health, don't waste time.

Your body has the ability to regenerate and heal itself, so never lose faith in your own recovery. If you work regularly in favor of your body, you will achieve your goals! Taking one step at a time will help you do away with your stress, depression, and anxiety. Exercise can be the bridge you have to cross until you finally achieve your goal and become a healthier and happier version of yourself!

You are worth each minute that you invest in yourself in order to transform your life for the better!

CHAPTER 11

Seeing in the Darkness

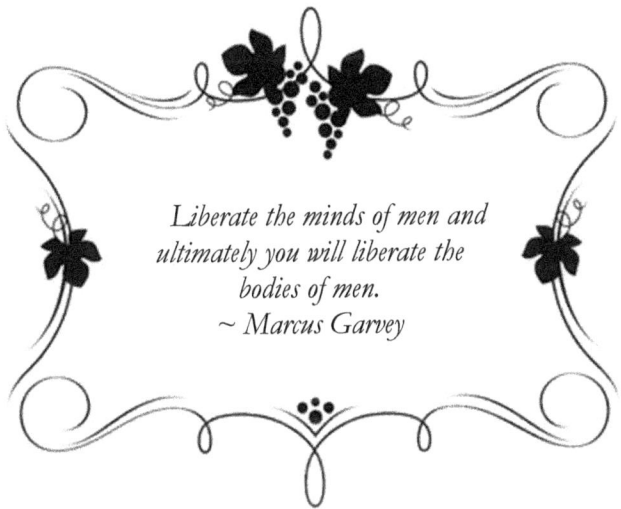

Liberate the minds of men and ultimately you will liberate the bodies of men.
~ Marcus Garvey

If you have been following this book's instructions and are still feeling overwhelmed by your problems and the symptoms of anxiety, believe me, there is hope.

As far as anxiety disorders are concerned, it has been proven that therapy is by far the most efficient solution to combating it. Unlike anxiety medication, which treats the symptoms of the problem, anxiety therapy provides natural but specialized sophisticated treatment. What it does is help you determine the causes of your worries and fears. It helps you reach deep relaxation, develop a fresh and comfortable look on everything *new*, as well as help you improve your coping skills and also your ability to solve your problems. It is an effective way to overcome anxiety by using the right tools.

As mentioned in the previous chapter, there are several types of anxiety disorders. Therapy has to be customized to your individual symptoms and concerns. For example, if you have obsessive-compulsive disorder, your treatment plan will differ from one used to treat panic disorders. Therapy is personalized and information such as the anxiety type and severity of the condition will determine its length. Even so, anxiety treatments typically don't last long. According to the American Psychological Association, eight to ten therapy sessions like Cognitive Behavioural Therapy (CBT) have proven to be sufficient to help many people improve their mental health significantly.

In the UK, the IAPT (Improving Access to Psychological Therapies) programme was created to offer "stress-free" admission to those in anxiety treatments through the NHS (National Health Service). It is easy and free. If you are living in the UK, ask your general practitioner and they will refer you to CBT or counselling services. However, if you feel uncomfortable asking your GP for these services, you can refer yourself for counselling services. The PCT (Primary Care Trust) allows you to go directly to the therapist through a self-referral. To learn more about what psychological therapy services are available in your area go to the NHS web site: www.nhs/ServiceSearch/Psychological%20therapies%(IAPT)/LocationSearch/10008

For those who live in the US, South Africa, Canada, and Australia, it is good to learn more about psychological therapy services available in your area; you can find website references at the end of this book. There you will find information about how mental health services work in your country, if it is free or private and what the best and closest services available for you are.

Anxiety can be treated with different approaches, but the most widely known and used are cognitive behavioural therapy and exposure therapy. Each therapy can be used as a separate treatment modality or combined with other treatments. It can be done alone in individual therapy or in a group of people who share similar anxiety issues.

Cognitive Behavioural Therapy

Cognitive behavioural therapy (CBT) is the leading therapy used to treat anxiety disorders. It has already proven efficient in the treatment of anxiety issues like panic disorder, phobias, social anxiety disorder as well as generalized anxiety disorder.

This therapy helps you deal with negative patterns that represent your outlook on the surrounding world and yourself. As you can grasp by its name, there are two main components of this approach:

Cognitive Therapy

Cognitive therapy puts an emphasis on examining negative thought patterns, also referred to as cognitions, and how they bring influences to the development of anxiety.

Behaviour Therapy

Behaviour therapy places an emphasis on examining your reactions in moments of anxiety.

What cognitive behavioural therapy argues is that our thought patterns determine the way we feel. External factors, such as events and circumstances, have no major value; it is your perception of them that ultimately affect how you feel. For instance, you've been invited to attend a big party. Give some thought to the three distinct ways you would feel about this invitation, and the way your thoughts would eventually affect your sensations.

Using the above example - a friend has just invited you to a big party. What will be the first thought that crosses your mind?

1. **Example of Thought:** It sounds that the part will be exciting. I love to have fun and interact with new people!
   - **Raised Emotions:** Excitement and happiness.

2. **Example of Thought:** I don't feel comfortable going around in public. I would rather stay home and watch TV.

    - **Raised Emotions:** Neutral, uncertainty.

3. **Example of Thought:** I am no good at socializing with others. I will make a fool of myself.

    - **Raised Emotions:** Fear and anxiety.

From these examples, you can observe that the same situation can stir up various emotions in different people and have different implications. Therefore, it is primarily based on individual self-esteem attitudes, beliefs and expectations. Those who suffer from anxiety disorders and negative thought patterns feel nervous when they are facing new and challenging situations. It triggers negative emotions that ultimately lead to feelings of frustration, fear and anxiety. The objective of CBT is to help you transform negative thought patterns and beliefs and gain a new perspective on the situation in question. By helping you to change your thoughts, you will change your feelings, actions and reactions. It really can change your reality.

The therapy does a cognitive rearrangement and it represents a more challenging process that helps restructure your negative thinking by replacing your negative thoughts with positive ones. There are three main steps to doing this:

1. Recognizing Your Negative Thoughts

In the case of anxiety disorders, you perceive some circumstances as threatening, though maybe you aren't aware of that. For example, to someone who suffers from germ phobia, the simple habit of shaking someone's hand can feel threatening and uncomfortable. Even though you can recognize this fear as being irrational, determining what your own scary and irrational thoughts are can be incredibly challenging. Ask yourself what thoughts you were having when your anxiety started. A

CHAPTER 11: Seeing in the Darkness

consultation with a therapist can help you identify the hidden thoughts in your mind.

2. Challenging Your Negative Thoughts

What your therapist will do is help you to identify and evaluate thoughts that trigger your fears. Such steps as realizing the realistic evidence for why you're bombarded with such thoughts, determining wrong beliefs as well as giving it a real life test of your negative expectations will be pursued. The solutions to help you deal with negative thinking are learning to analyse the pros and cons of your worries and genuinely identifying the chances of your worries or fears turning into reality or not.

3. The Substitution of Negative Thoughts with Realistic Views

As soon as you realise that irrational predictions, together with negative distortions, are triggering your anxiety and provoking thoughts, you will be able to transform them into positive ones with a higher rate of accuracy and positivity. Your therapist will also provide you with calming and soothing statements that will comfort you in your reality. You will be able to tell them to yourself whenever your anxiety levels rise up.

Changing your thought patterns is not as easy as it might seem! Often, negative thoughts have a deep root because of accumulated negative thinking during an entire lifetime. It requires practice to break the habit. The therapist will give you some lessons to practice at home to control the anxiety disorder.

Cognitive behaviour therapy may also include:

Identifying the exact moment when you get anxious and the processes surrounding it

- Developing coping skills and learning efficient relaxation techniques in combating anxiety and panic disorders

- Confronting your fears (It doesn't matter whether it is in your imagination or in real life.)

Many people suffering from anxiety avoid situations that may cause anxiety. For example, if you fear altitudes, you might end up driving three hours to avoid crossing a tall bridge. Another example would be if you get panicky at the thought of giving a speech in public, you might as well avoid it by not going to your best friend's wedding. Besides feeling high discomfort in this situation, there is also the difficulty of overcoming the fears, which never happens when you avoid them. More than that, concerns tend to get more powerful when you avoid them.

Exposure Therapy

Exposure therapy, as you can guess, has you meet the things or objects you fear face-to-face. It is believed that repetitively performing an uncomfortable action or exposing you to the phobia or anxiety-inducer will help you to achieve a certain level of confidence and control over the situation. As a result, your anxiety will diminish. It can be conducted in two main ways: your therapist may advise you to visualise a scary situation or you might have to deal with it face-to-face. Exposure therapy can be used as a separate treatment or as part of cognitive behavioural therapy.

Exposure therapy puts an emphasis on gradual exposure to your biggest fear. Otherwise, it might turn out to be very traumatizing. This kind of approach is known as systematic desensitisation. What this approach does is help you confront your fears step-by-step, along with increasing your self-confidence and perfecting your panic controlling skills.

It is conducted in three parts. For example, on the fear of flying we will have:

- **Step 1:** Getting accustomed to looking at pictures of an aeroplane
- **Step 2:** Watching videos that give you the motivation to get in the aeroplane (avoid those with aeroplane crashes)
- **Step 3:** Watching real aeroplanes at the airport
- **Step 4:** Booking a ticket
- **Step 5:** Checking in for your flight
- **Step 6:** Waiting for boarding
- **Step 7:** Taking your seat
- **Step 8:** Taking the flight

Your therapist will teach you step by step how to overcome the fear and also some relaxation techniques, using deep breathing and relaxation. Exercises to relax can be performed in both therapy sessions and at home as well.

As soon as you start challenging your fears, this may trigger some physical anxiety response and trembling or hyperventilation can occur. However, the therapist will guide you towards a deep relaxation state.

The next step involve making up a list of ten to twenty situations you find scary, which aim to help you reach your final goal. As an example, looking at photos of planes or eventually taking a short flight can help; you reduce or battle your fear of flying. However, remember that steps have to be carried out gradually and as accurately as possible to reach clear signs of improvement.

The third step will consist of working with your list under the instructions of your therapist. Your primary goal is to control yourself until your fears begin to diminish. These are how you are going to perceive those feelings that don't have an external power over you and they have the tendency to leave after a while. You will use the relaxation techniques taught at therapy sessions whenever you feel anxiety episodes soaring up. Besides, as soon as you reach relaxation, you will be able to work on the situation again. The key here is completing all the tasks without overwhelming yourself.

The exploration of your anxiety issues can also be treated with complementary therapies intended to decrease your stress levels and help you to regain emotional balance.

Relaxation Techniques

Relaxation techniques such as mindfulness meditation, controlled breathing, visualization and progressive muscle relaxation can produce significant improvements with your anxiety issue and can help you establish a powerful emotional balance within yourself.

Biofeedback

Biofeedback measures your physiological response to anxiety. This therapy makes use of specific sensors that monitor your physiological functions — heart rate, muscle tension and breathing. It allows you to understand and perceive your body's anxiety response and teaches you to effectively use relaxation techniques to take control and relax.

Undoubtedly, anxiety isn't a condition you can treat in a very short period. To effectively combat anxiety disorders, you must be patient and commit to the journey. Don't forget that therapy includes confronting your fears face-to-face; therefore, there might be moments when you feel much worse before the treatment starts to work. It is of enormous importance that you follow the treatment and listen to the advice given by your therapist. Whenever you have those moments where you feel discouraged by the length of the treatment, you should always remember that therapy is proven to deliver impressive results. You will achieve your final goal if you commit and have some

CHAPTER 11: Seeing in the Darkness

patience. Adhering to positive life choices described in this book will reduce the treatment's length and increase satisfaction with the results.

CHAPTER 12

Anaesthesia for the Pain

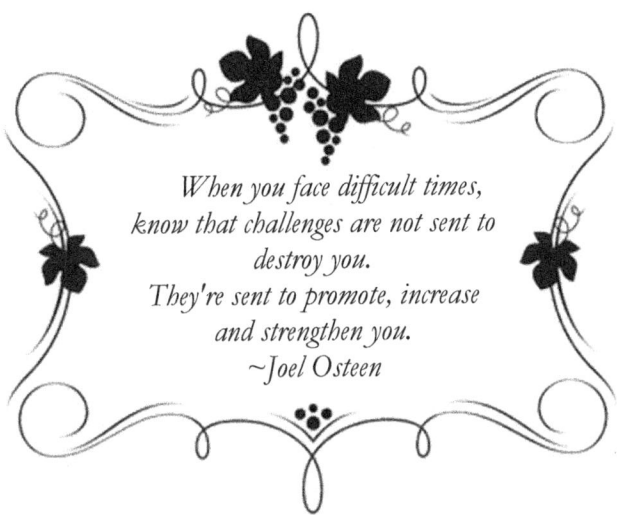

*When you face difficult times, know that challenges are not sent to destroy you.
They're sent to promote, increase and strengthen you.*
~Joel Osteen

If you still find it hard to get out from depression or anxiety, it's crucial that you consider the risks of anxiety medication, because they can trigger a number of undesirable, even dangerous, adverse effects. Recent work published by Harvard University concluded that it is fundamental that your doctor asks for a hormonal evaluation (blood test) before prescribing any antidepressant to treat mental conditions such as anxiety and depression.

According to the Harvard scientists, hormone fluctuations can cause mood disorders and depression. Now tell me, can you guess how many physicians carried out a test on my hormone levels? None! I didn't have the pleasure of meeting a single physician that did, and I visited many of them. It looks that, they have never worked with the Harvard guidelines. However, a good physician after analysing your hormones, will decide if it is necessary to adjust you hormone levels, in the worst-case scenario, a good physicians or psychiatrists will recommend you to use hormone modulation before prescribing antidepressants.

Hormone modulations in my opinion are safe and healthy way to balance your hormones, because they are a bio-identical hormone replacement therapies. After many studies, I discovered that one of the reasons for my depression was thyroid malfunction. However, instead of using hormone modulation, a simple supplementation with iodine, vitamin B_3 and vitamin B_2 to support my thyroid functions made my levels of energy come back in full potency and the symptoms of depression were gone completely. I am sure that many people diagnosed with anxiety or depression are in the same situation as I was without being aware of it.

Antidepressants, with an accurate diagnosis and if correctly administered, may have a positive effect in the short run to alleviate patients' severe anxiety and depression symptoms. However, they shouldn't be viewed as the path to cure, because they don't heal the underlying cause of the anxiety disorder. Usually, when you are taking antidepressants, as soon as you stop taking the drug, all symptoms resurface in full potency.

Anxiety medication surely won't provide help when you're confronting such a distressing thing as mounting bills or an unhealthy relationship. In this case, therapy and lifestyle changes can work more efficiently alone or in conjunction with the medication. Moreover, a lot of medication for anxiety can be physically addictive, which will make it difficult to stop using them.

Tranquilizers are often used to relieve anxiety and are efficient medications that work by slowing down the central nervous system, what has made them genuinely popular are their calming and relaxing properties. However, some substances used in antidepressant pills work in the opposite direction, poisoning your neurons, so be careful. In the case of

CHAPTER 12: Anaesthesia for the Pain

anxiety, they may be the number one choice. Many times, they might also be prescribed as muscle relaxants or for better sleep.

You may recognise these drugs as:

- Klonopin also known as clonazepam
- Valium also known as diazepam
- Xanax also known as alprazolam
- Ativan also known as lorazepam

Some medications, such as benzodiazepines, are fast-acting, commonly alleviating anxiety within thirty minutes to an hour. Considering that, they act quickly, benzodiazepines are ideal for preventing a panic attack or any other suddenly distressing anxiety episodes. However, this type of medication operates by slowing down brain activity, because of this it can bring undesirable side effects. The higher the dose of this drug, the greater the impact the side effects on your mind and body will be. When you are under the influence of this drug you may suddenly feel sleepy, become uncoordinated, feel forgetful or have a foggy brain (even if you take a small dosage of benzodiazepines). It can make everyday activities difficult to manage, such as work, school or even driving. Medication hangover is an undesirable effect you might feel the next day upon waking up.

Your body metabolizes benzodiazepines slowly. In addition, these kind of pills have to be present in the body for long periods of time. When used for extended periods, over-sedation is a common complication. Those who feel over sedated might act or look like they are drunk and exhibit any of the following signs:

- Weakness
- Indistinct Speech
- Confusion or Disorientation
- Depression
- Memory Issues

- Nausea
- Dizziness
- Blurred or Double Vision

The higher the dosage, the greater the risk of developing severe depressive symptoms coupled with suicidal thoughts. More than that, emotional blunting or numbness is a common health implication. Therefore, while these medications alleviate anxiety, they also block feelings of pain or pleasure.

Paradoxical excitement can also be another side effect of anti-anxiety medication. Such may include heightened anxiety, agitation, and irritability. A host of side effects from aggravated anxiety can include:

- Obsession
- Aggression and anger
- Hallucinations
- Impulsive behaviour

The pills' paradoxical reactions usually occur in children, elderly and people with developmental disabilities. When it comes to depression, many medications have been permitted by NICE-UK (National Institute for Health and Care Excellence). There are many medications used to treat depression including selective Serotonin Reuptake Inhibitors (SSRIs), Tricyclic Antidepressants (TCAs), Monoamine Oxidase Inhibitors (MAOIs) as well as atypical antidepressants.

In the treatment of anxiety, antidepressants are usually preferred over traditional anti-anxiety drugs, mainly because of the lower risk of dependence or abuse. Even so, to begin seeing results, you will want to use the medication for up to four to six weeks. They do not act fast, and in the case of a panic attack, they do not help much. In the case of chronic anxiety, such medications focus on relieving some of the symptoms needing an on-going treatment.

CHAPTER 12: Anaesthesia for the Pain

The drugs commonly prescribed in the treatment of anxiety are SSRIs including Prozac, Zoloft, Paxil, Lexapro and Celexa. The intention of these drugs is to regulate serotonin levels in the brain, positively influencing the mood. Unfortunately, in the majority of cases it doesn't happen. Such medications are often used in the treatment of panic disorder, OCD and GAD.

As I said before, some substances are highly addictive. Some may take some time to develop physical dependence on the antidepressant, but it still has significant concerns, such as withdrawal. Whenever you discontinue the treatment aprompty, you might experience antidepressant withdrawal, which is usually accompanied by such symptoms as deep depression, fatigue, anxiety, irritability, flu-like symptoms and insomnia.

NICE-UK requires all manufacturers of antidepressants to disclose warning signs regarding the high risk of suicidal thoughts, agitation as well as hostility. Other concern about antidepressants are that most of them may elevate instead of decrease depression or anxiety symptoms, especially in adolescents.

The same antidepressant can be used differently, according to the country. For example, Buspirone is globally used as an anti-anxiety drug. It has mild tranquilizing properties. However, its application differs between countries. For example, in the UK, it is used for short-term treatment only. However, in the US, the FDA approved this drug for both long and short-term anxiety. It is prescribed to alleviate anxiety symptoms by elevating serotonin levels in the brain, just like the SSRIs, as well as by lowering dopamine levels. In comparison to traditional anti-anxiety drugs like Xanax, Buspirone is slow acting. It will take up to two weeks to start showing results compared to thirty minutes for benzodiazepines.

Typical adverse reactions of Buspirone may include:

- Nausea
- Headaches

- Dizziness
- Lethargy
- Constipation

Nevertheless, it does provide good results in the case of GAD, but in other instances of anxiety, CBT therapy seems to be more effective.

Beta-blockers are the medications used in the treatment of high blood pressure as well as heart issues. Even so, they are usually prescribed as an off-label treatment for anxiety. They operate primarily by blocking the outcomes of norepinephrine, which is a stress hormone used in the fight-or-flight response. They provide good management of physical symptoms like increased heart rate, trembling voice, dizziness and sweating coupled with shaky hands.

Beta-blockers are usually used in the treatment of phobias (mainly social phobia and performance anxiety), primarily because of their effectiveness in dealing with such emotional symptoms as worry. Therefore, if you take a beta-blocker whenever you find yourself anticipating a big event, you may be able to calm your nerves a bit.

Such drugs as Propranolol (Inderal) and Atenolol (Tenormin) are common beta-blockers. They include such effects as:

- Vertigo
- Fatigue
- Slow pulse
- Nausea

Aside from the typical side effects, they can also trigger severe complications if used in combination with other substances, such as prescription painkillers, alcohol or even sleeping pills. When this happens, the effect may be deadly. Life-threatening drug interactions may also happen whenever the patient takes anti-anxiety drugs together with antihistamines,

CHAPTER 12: Anaesthesia for the Pain

used to relieve cold and allergy symptoms as well as provide better sleep.

Toxicity can also be increased by consuming such antidepressants as Zoloft or Prozac. Therefore, it is mandatory that you speak with your doctor or pharmacist prior to subjecting yourself to any particular combination of medications.

Anyone using anti-anxiety medication can encounter undesirable or even threatening side effects. However, the potential dangers are greater for seniors over sixty-five years of age, pregnant women and those with a history of substance abuse because it can trigger their addiction and lead them to abuse, especially when used in an unsafe mixture with alcohol or other drugs.

Before you choose the medication to treat your anxiety disorder, it is very important to gather as much information on your prescription drug as possible, rather than use it blindly. The more information you have at your disposal, the easier it will be for you to identify and cope with side effects, prevent life-threatening drug interactions and lower other medication risks.

A few suggestions for those of you considering taking anxiety medication:

- Have patience, avoid the consumption of alcohol, document your reaction to new medications or dosage, consult with your healthcare practitioners and never suddenly cease therapy without checking with your provider.

- Always remind yourself that anti-anxiety medications should be used as a short-term remedy. Despite the downfall of long-term use, many people continue to use it over extended periods. This can be dangerous because certain medications, such as benzodiazepines, may quickly result in physical dependency. You can also develop a drug tolerance, requiring that you up your dose just to find the same levels of anxiety relief.

A large number of people develop addictions within just a few months of consuming some anti-anxiety drugs. Moreover, as soon as you get physically dependent on any anxiety medication, it's very hard to cease taking it. The body feels accustomed to the drug and you can experience withdrawal symptoms whenever the dose is decreased or the treatment is discontinued. There is also such a thing as psychological dependence, and it may cause issues, too. You might lose confidence in yourself and your capacity to do away with life's difficulties by beginning to believe that this medication is the only thing that can keep you alive.

If you are already using any anti-anxiety drugs and have already become physically dependent on this medication and think it is time to cease the treatment, you'll have to get the guidance of your health care practitioner. It is critical that the dose is gradually decreased over a specified period to ensure you don't experience a withdrawal reaction. However, if you have been taking the medication for a couple of months, withdrawal symptoms also may occur. Moreover, such symptoms as anxiety, depression or insomnia may last over an extended period for months after stopping the medication. Regrettably, such effects are usually confused with the return of the anxiety disorder, which is why the majority of people restart the medication all over again.

As mentioned before, there are more widely accepted and efficient alternative ways to treat anxiety instead of medication, such as therapy. Nevertheless, to truly do away with anxiety once and for all, you must also make significant changes to your lifestyle, even if you choose therapy or prescription drugs. Lifestyle adjustments are a great help, so maybe it is time to have a closer look at your overall daily routine, from dysfunctional sleeping patterns to whether you are getting

CHAPTER 12: Anaesthesia for the Pain

regular exercise and consuming a healthy diet. There are other good complementary or alternative treatments for anxiety, such as supplements, hypnosis, acupuncture, meditation and biofeedback.

It is good to be reminded that the primary benefit of avoiding drug treatments for anxiety is that alternative therapies are centred on long-lasting relief. Medication may be adequate; however, its benefits may be short-lived for controlling your symptoms of anxiety. In case of severe anxiety or depression, once your anxiety symptoms are under control, it is helpful to consider others forms of therapy to manage them. This is the key to increasing well-being and overall health.

CHAPTER 13

The Gain From the Pain

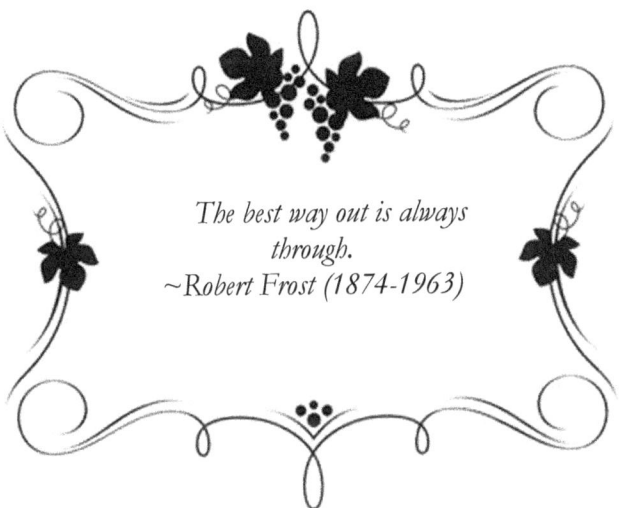

The best way out is always through.
~Robert Frost (1874-1963)

You may experience the full gamut of emotions during a lifetime. Regrettably, there's no good without the bad. Therefore, there's little chance you'll circumvent a loss of someone or something you love. Life is unpredictable. It is black and white, sweet and sour—all at the same time. Maybe you have already been subjected to pain and deep sadness from events that happened in the past or are happening right now, and they have somehow transformed whom you are in the present day.

Life presents us a balance between positivity and negativity. But remember, no matter how bad you may feel in the moment, difficult moments can bring you the opportunity to teach a lesson and contribute significantly to your growth and to others lives. Be confident that there's always going to be a light at the end of the tunnel. Be patient and you will find it.

Grief is one of the most negative and unpleasant emotions you may feel at any time in your life. When it occurs, it is a time to *reboot*. Listen to your heart, quietly. It is necessary to face the pain with maturity in order to heal.

What is Grief?

Grief is the normal reaction we experience when facing a loss. It is an emotional response when we feel *vulnerable*. It is a form of suffering when something or someone we love is taken away from us.

Grief can be a result of many life happenings, such as:

- Loss or death of a beloved one
- Relationship breakup or divorce
- Serious disease of a loved one
- Loss of financial stability
- Loss of security after trauma
- Severe disease or diagnosis with terminal illness
- Sudden loss of a significant job
- Loss or death of a pet
- And many more

Grief is one of the most complicated and detrimental emotions you can experience. There is no right or wrong in the grieving process; everyone grieves in a different way because it is extremely individual. Your response to the pain is based on many factors, such as your personality, experiences, your environment, your culture, faith and your coping skills.

The healing process takes time. It occurs gradually and cannot be forced or hurried. Some people feel better in just few weeks; others may need months to recover. For others, it can take years. If you are experiencing grief right now or know someone who is grieving, the key words here are *patience* and *understanding*. Respecting the person's time, the healing process is crucial.

CHAPTER 13: The Gain From the Pain

Loss of a Beloved

It is very painful when we face the loss of someone who we really care about and love. If you are in this situation right now, the best advice I can give you is not to grieve alone. Allow people to come to you, talk with them about your feelings, your pain and your fears. Even if you have a hard time talking about your feelings, sharing your pain and opening your heart, it facilitates the healing process. Accepting and receiving support from friends and family supplements your own coping skills, and may provide just the strength you need to avoid the "extra help" of antidepressants and sleeping pills. When you accept and receive support from friends and family, you receive greater strength for coping with the loss.

Relationship Breakup or Divorce

Romantic relationships start full of excitement and expectations for the future. The lovers live to please each other. However, for some couples, the appreciation in being together ends. An exchange of offences replaces words of love, and instead of laughs, there are just pain and tears. When the relationship fails, we feel profound disappointment, distress and grief.

It is sad, but sometimes it is hard to understand why two good people no longer share the same expectations and dreams, no matter how much energy and time they had dedicated to each other, even if they've done their best, they now blame each other for unhappiness or failure, and they realize that they no longer desire to remain together, it's time to go. Appreciating each other's past efforts and using all that they have learnt will help to value future relationships without guilt or blame.

When you have a relationship breakup or divorce, everything is disrupted: your home, your responsibilities, your routine and your relationships with friends and extended family. All these changes can confuse your identity. It also includes multiples losses:

- Companionship
- Support (emotional, financial, social, intellectual)
- Hopes and dreams

When your relationship ends, many questions come to mind: How will your life be without your partner? Is there someone else in this world for you? Will you end up by yourself?

All these questions frequently sound worse than staying in a relationship, even when the relationship no longer serves you well.

It is normal to feel scared when facing uncertainties. You may feel that you will be unable to bear these intense emotions; remember that grieving is necessary for the healing process. The pain of grief is exactly what helps you let go of the old relationship and move forward. The death of love is one of the hardest experiences, and no matter how strong your pain is, remember that it won't last forever.

What You Need to Know About Grief

The more you understand about the grief process, the more prepared you will be to help a grieving friend or family member.

As mentioned earlier, grief affects people in different ways. The most common symptoms of grief include:

- **Going into shock** – Soon after a loss, it can be hard to accept what happened. Feeling numb or as if you are living inside a nightmare is normal.

- **Sadness** – Profound and continuous sadness might be the universally experienced symptom for those dealing with grief. Typically, profound sadness can also be accompanied by feelings of despair, loneliness and emptiness. At this stage, you feel very emotional, and cry easily. This is also considered normal.

- **Anger** – You might experience anger when you grieve. Moreover, this can be accompanied by resentfulness and feelings of abandonment. It is normal to feel the need to get answers about what happened and to blame someone for the unfairness that was done to you. You may feel angry with yourself, the doctors, God, with your partner or with the person that abandoned you.

- **Uncertainty** – You may feel insecurity, with fears of the future and indecision about what way to go, what to do and how to overcome the pain.

- **Guilt** – Many people suffering from grief experience the feeling of guilt. This guilt may not have a solid foundation. However, it is normal to feel guilty for things you've done, for things you haven't done and/or things you've said or didn't have the chance to say.

- **Fear** – The pain of grief can open doors for anxiety disorders, such as panic attacks or severe anxiety, accompanied by heart palpitations and feelings of constant stress.

- **Nausea and fatigue** – Physical symptoms may also appear in the majority of cases because the emotional stress is so strong that it can involve physical symptoms, such as insomnia, pains, weight gain or loss, nausea, faint, fatigue, appetite loss and lowered immunity.

As mentioned, it is very important that you have patience and respect the time needed to heal. However, there are some things that can make the process a bit easier. I am going to provide you with a few ideas that can help you in the path toward healing:

- **Get support from friends and family** - As mentioned before, it is very important not to be alone when in intense emotional pain. Share your feelings and fears with others; it will help you to *empty* your heart. Give others the chance to help you. Remember that the time spent with friends and family is priceless, and it is a good step for rehabilitating your broken heart and soul.

- **Nourish your soul** - If you follow a spiritual belief, embrace the comfort it can provide you. Meditation, prayer or going to church can help. If your pain is making you feel confused about your faith, talk to a clergy member or other trusted leaders in your community.

- **Find a support group** - The grief may make you feel isolated. Sometimes even when you have others around you, you can feel misunderstood; sharing your pain with those who have experienced similar losses can help. Churches, hospitals, hospices and counselling centres in your area may have bereavement support groups; it is a good idea to try to contact them.

In London, there is a group of volunteers named Compassionate Neighbours that offers emotional support, companionship and a listening ear. They also direct you to other important support services to help you overcome challenging times. I know that this initiative is available in many other communities across the world. You can Google it and find out about similar services near you. If you are in London, you can find more information about Compassionate Neighbours at the website at www.stjh.org.uk/neighbours.

What to Do When the Grief Pain Becomes Unbearable

The pain of losing a loved one never goes away completely. However, if you feel stuck in continuous and intense pain, maybe you are suffering from a state called complicated grief. It happens when there is no acceptance of the loss. This occurs when a person is still fixated on their loss even after long periods of time and it continues to disrupt their daily routine.

The symptoms of complicated grief are:

- Denial of the loss (death or relationship breakup)
- Searching for the person in familiar places
- Extreme resentment over the loss
- Avoiding things that remind you of your loved one

It is not easy to identify the difference between depression or complicated grief, because their symptoms are often similar. The principal difference is that with complicated grief, you have ups and downs, and with time you will experience pleasure and contentment. The symptoms of depression, such as lack of vitality, hopelessness and desolation, are continuous.

Getting Professional Help for Grief

It is necessary to seek professional support when you recognize the symptoms. Untreated, complicated grief can cause emotional damage, physical health problems and even suicide.

Contact a doctor or a therapist if you:

- Feel hopeless and don't see any reason for living
- Feel disconnected from others a long time after the loss
- Feel difficulty trusting others
- Feel guilt for the loss

During my life, I have had the opportunity to meet some extraordinary people. A few of them caught my attention in a very special way, because they not only overcame the pain of grief, but taught us a wonderful lesson from their experiences. In this chapter, I am going to share the stories of two amazing women. They will share with us their experiences with grief, and how they overcame it, and what they have learnt from that episode.

Wendy's Story

Wendy is a wonderful woman, and when I met her for the first time, I realized that I had a great deal to learn from her. I try to be near her as often as possible. She is a role model of generosity and kindness. Wendy is full of life, and she shares that energy with everyone and everything in her orbit. There is no way to avoid being touched by her selflessness and warmth. Because of that, I asked her to share her experiences with my readers.

Wendy uses the words soulmate, business partner, and husband to define how significant John was to her. She will share with us her feelings and fears when her husband was unexpectedly diagnosed with brain cancer, and how she coped with this life-changing event.

Her Reaction to the Bad News

John and I were on holiday when he started having violent headaches. We both knew something was wrong; he never suffered from headaches. He became quiet and withdrawn, which was completely out of his character. Typically, John was a cheerful person who loved every moment of his life. We telephoned a doctor, who sent us immediately to the nearest hospital; within twenty-four hours, John had every imaginable test and was diagnosed with a brain tumour, which the neurologist deemed "inoperable." He treated John with steroids to reduce the swelling and wouldn't discharge him until a travelling nurse had been secured and an appointment with a London neurosurgeon had been confirmed.

CHAPTER 13: The Gain From the Pain

I am a fairly calm, matter-of-fact person, but I think I was in shock. Reality didn't sink in for several days, and neither of us really understood what it all meant. We both stayed positive, and John was convinced that he was going to get better.

How Wendy Coped During John's Illness

We flew back to England and, after a couple of hours rest at home, we went to Charing Cross Hospital, where we met Mr Kevin O'Neill (Neurosurgeon and Brain Tumour Specialist). He came in on August Bank Holiday Monday! Within a few days, John had an eight-hour operation to remove 90% of the tumour, which was deemed to be a Grade IV astrocytoma—the worst possible diagnosis. We were told it was incurable but with aggressive radiotherapy, there was a good chance his life could be extended, and John remained positive throughout. I followed his lead, although in my heart of hearts I think I knew he was going to die. We never once discussed death, and always talked about him getting better, concentrating on enjoying life to the fullest despite his illness.

He wanted to go back to work the day following surgery, and while he was having radiotherapy, he would go to work and then come back after an hour's nap.

He had a blood disorder, which caused several complications, so he was in and out of hospital quite often and sometimes got confused and frustrated by occasional short-term memory loss. Then in May (nine months after the diagnosis), he began losing strength on his left side, and his memory got worse. He would forget what he was saying halfway through a sentence. One night he fell out of bed and I couldn't get him back up again. I knew we couldn't cope on our own, so I called an ambulance to take him to the hospital. He believed it was a temporary move – he had just started taking temozolomide as part of a clinical trial and had been told that things would get worse before they got better. One day, he closed his eyes and never opened them again. He never spoke again, nor reacted in any way. We never got to say goodbye and I never knew if he had just given up or was waiting until "the worst was over".

We were very fortunate to have a fantastic team at the office who kept the business going while we dealt with the illness; I was able to look after him whenever needed. If you ask me how I coped, I honestly don't know – I just did!

Wendy's Feelings When Her Husband Died

I was very lucky to have a wonderful group of friends who "scooped me up" when John died – part of me was glad the wait was over after one week into the coma. The other part of me was numb and lost. I have no idea how I got through all the administrative formalities, but I know I could not have done it without the help of my friends. As John and I were business partners as well as soulmates, husband and wife and best friends, we had our employees to support us, too. They helped to organise his funeral, notify all of our clients, suppliers, friends and industry colleagues.

Over 350 people came to his funeral while I was still on autopilot. I don't even know when reality started to kick in. Like John, I fell back on the things that mattered most – the business, our employees and my friends who were always there for me to lean on and keep me from being alone and falling apart. We had been in the process of selling our flat and buying a new one when he was ill, so I had to make a big decision whether to go ahead with the move or stay put. In the end, I decided that it was what John would have wanted. I busied myself with clearing out his things quickly and getting on with the move. This probably helped to keep me busy and get through the time immediately after his death – if in doubt I always keep myself busy rather than dwell on my sadness.

What Wendy Learnt From the Experience

They say that people usually go through the full gamut of feelings when they lose a loved one, but the one emotion that I never had was anger – everything else, but no anger. One of the

CHAPTER 13: The Gain From the Pain

lasting lessons I learnt from this experience is the absolute waste of negative energy. I try to avoid it at all costs; there is nothing more destructive and pointless!

I quickly learnt how much everyone else had loved John the way I did, and I was overwhelmed by the support I received (as well as the £13,000 that was given to the research fund I had set up with Kevin's help). I realised quickly that I needed another purpose in my life after John's death, and the idea of continuing to fund the desperately-needed research into brain tumours that Kevin had told me about slowly blossomed into the creation of our charity, the Brain Tumour Research Campaign. When people say how wonderful I am (how magnanimous and generous) I know that, in reality, I was doing it for myself – perhaps even to keep myself sane! It was some time later that I understood that I was not only helping myself, but also giving those who loved John a way to express their love for him and do something concrete to relieve their own grief and sorrow at his loss. And of course, I felt able to make something good come from something bad and help others where we couldn't help John.

What Gave Wendy Hope and the Power to Overcome Her Grief

I wish I could say that my faith gave me the hope and strength to carry on, but I would be lying. Indeed, I have always said that God and I had agreed to a difference of opinion over John's death, and I felt He had turned away from us and betrayed us both.

It was my friends, old and new – those who had known us both and shared my loss, and those I met in the brain tumour community I had joined – who kept (and continue to keep) me going. And the knowledge that what I am doing is creating a living legacy for my beloved husband who loved life and lived it to the fullest. I know he would be incredibly proud of what we have created and achieved. I do it for John.

Antidepressants

When I asked Wendy about her painful experience and whether she used any antidepressant to help her cope with her pain, she responded with "No, I didn't take any medication at all, just herbal Rescue Remedy."

On the back of this book, you are going to find more information about Wendy and the charity Mr Kevin and Wendy are working with – Brain Tumour Research.

Marina's Story

Marina is an extraordinary woman, and when I first met her, a life lesson begun. She is full of enthusiasm for life and her energy and kindness are contagious. I love to be around her; it is time guaranteed to be filled with loud laughs. For this reason, I asked her to share her experiences with my readers. She is going to share with us her feelings, fears, and uncertainty during her marriage and divorce. It occurred in a period when divorced women were harshly discriminated against by society, and she will share how she coped with it all.

Marina is a Brazilian woman who was born into a large family of six sisters and one brother. There was a deep bond between them all. As a teenager, Marina had many dreams –the most important of which was marriage, children and daily happiness. She was very young when she fell in love with a man that she thought was her soulmate. They married shortly after their first meeting.

With time, she began to notice that cultural differences were creating barriers between them. She came from a large Italian family, matriarchal and emotionally close; he came from a patriarchal family and grew up in the Japanese tradition. From the beginning, Marina showed interest in learning a new culture,

CHAPTER 13: The Gain From the Pain

trying her best to please her husband and to adapting to a married life. The cultural distance between them caused her to enter into an inner conflict, and she began to feel a deep sadness. The births of her children led to the hope that, with time, everything would get better. Despite her dedication as a wife and mother, she says that she never felt loved by her husband.

She feared the shame of being divorced and of being rejected by society. These fears prolonged her days as a wife and of feeling fragile and unhappy in her marriage.

One day, Marina decided to give herself some space from her relationship, so she travelled to her sister's house in another country for a three-month holiday with her children. During the period she was away from her husband, she became certain that the love she had for her husband was no longer in her heart. When she returned home, she started the process of legal separation. It was a stressful time, and Marina suffered with complete physical and mental exhaustion. She describes that as a "very difficult phase." The divorce greatly increased her responsibilities as a mother, because she and her kids were living in a different and distant city from her ex-husband. She says that, little by little, her confidence and her life improved. Ultimately, the feelings that remained between her ex-husband and her were simply mutual respect.

Sad news came when everything seemed to be under control – her ex-husband was seriously ill. The fear of death made him rethink the values of life and all he had left to live for. So, unexpectedly, he asked Marina to marry him for the second time. After a long time of consideration and despite being in a dilemma, she agreed. Marina believed that the decision could help him in his recovery process.

Exactly one year later, after she remarried him, he lost his battle with cancer and died.

She became depressed again, and pondered the many questions about life and death.

A few months following her husband's death, she also lost her sister to cancer. Again, she felt helpless. In 2014, her beloved mother passed away and, a few months after her mother's death, her only brother died. Because both deaths were recent, the pain was still great and during my interview with her, when Marina thought about her mother and brother, she paused to contain her tears.

She completed the interview by saying, "Life isn't easy, and it is so hard to be happy, especially when you bring with you the pain of the loss of your loved ones."

However, it is the love of her daughter and son that sustains her and, because of them, she tries her best to keep going and remain strong.

Her daughter was eight and her son ten when she got divorced. Alone, she supported both of her children to pursue their aspirations – degrees in medicine. Now Marina is sixty-five and lives in London, England. She is a very busy woman. She is facing the challenges of learning a new language, English. She attends school daily and, occasionally, adds classes in Italian. She feels very blessed now with the birth of her first grandchild, a beautiful boy!

Even with so many ups and downs in her life, she remains strong, loves life and shines her bright light upon us.

Marina did use antidepressants to help with her pain. However, after a more thorough check-up by her doctor, it was discovered that one reason for her depression was caused by a thyroid malfunction.

If you would like to contact Marina to ask any question or share your experience with her, you can do through the email at: marifavero@yahoo.it.

CHAPTER 13: The Gain From the Pain

My Story

I was born in Brazil, in a poor neighbourhood of São Paulo. I am the only child of my parents' failed marriage. At an early age, I understood that I was powerless regarding the choices of others. I grew up in a house where physical violence, shouting and offenses were part of my daily routine.

I was a sad and scared child, and my ambitious childhood dream was only to live in a peaceful house; to feel protected and loved. I spent my childhood and teen years hiding myself from my father. He didn't look at me through the eyes of a loving father; his intentions were clearly of a different nature. He tried to rape me many times. I was ashamed of being myself and simply wanted to be invisible. The fear, the shame, the self-hatred led me to believe that I should stay away from my home. My parents were very strict and they didn't allow me to go anywhere except to school, so I started studying as much as I could. Besides my regular classes, I completed many extra courses: English, manicuring, cooking, sewing, computing and crafts. No matter what it was, the important thing for me was to stay busy and away from my house.

Unfortunately, education isn't a priority to Brazil's government. Public schools are overcrowded, and it is very complicated for even skilled and well-intentioned teachers to make significant progress with students. I suffered a lot during the primary and secondary school. My academic history was based on poor performance in a very poor quality educational model.

When I was fifteen, I got a place in a new pilot project school called CEFAM-3 (unfortunately, this project had a short life, and few people were as fortunate as me). The government was offering a 4-year intensive training course to be a primary school teacher. It was one of the luckiest days of my life! There were small classes, a well-structured school and very highly skilled teachers offering not just knowledge but understanding and love. That school was my favourite place to be. There I felt important as a person, and my confidence started to develop and was demonstrated in my outstanding academic performance. There I learnt many subjects, such as psychology, methodologies, didactic, pedagogy and many others at a deeper level. I realised the importance of education as a tool to life transformation. I also discovered that teaching was my passion; I wanted to somehow make a difference in other lives, especially those who were innocent and misunderstood, as I had been. I started my mission as a teacher with inclinations toward intellectually challenged learning, such as dyslexia and demanding behaviour.

When I was nineteen, I started my first university course in psychology. I acquired a strong foundation in medicine, studying subjects such as anatomy (theory and practice on cadavers), physiology, biology, neurology, psychopathology and psychopharmacology. Suddenly, during my first year of undergraduate course, my mum had a massive stroke and, after one week in a coma, she died.

At my mum's funeral, I saw my inappropriately happy father, who introduced me to an unknown woman. He said that she would be my new "mother". I felt devastated with my father's insensitivity. All these years later, when I recall those memories, I have no words to express my feelings in relation to that event. I felt like I was stuck in an endless nightmare.

My feelings for my father were repugnance and repulsion. I felt ashamed for my mother. The man she loved so wholeheartedly, cared for and dedicated herself to for twenty-four years, hadn't deserved twenty-four seconds of her time.

CHAPTER 13: The Gain From the Pain

A few days later, that woman moved into my house. When I came back home from work, I was shocked to find her there. I felt enormous sadness, and the sense of shame from the neighbours were just a few of the sentiments I had on that day. When I saw the belongings of that stranger replacing my mother's things in my house, I didn't think twice. I picked up a few items of clothing and packed what I had and left to find another place to live.

Things in my life changed very quickly. I tried hard, but after a few months, I felt like I was still in shock; my sleep was completely disturbed, my mind started working as if it were in *slow motion*. I kept myself very busy to avoid thinking too much, working and studying as much as I could. However, even being on "automatic pilot," didn't help and I started having a physical breakdown. I lost my appetite; I tried to eat, but I was frequently sick to my stomach, and because of that, I lost ten kilos in just two months and I became very gaunt and undernourished.

I recognised that I was feeling very bad mentally and physically and I asked for help. I visited many doctors and they gave me antidepressants and sleeping pills. I felt glad because at the time I saw the pills as the only solution to take me out of that situation. However, I got worse and I received the diagnosis of severe depression. My memory was terrible. It is hard to explain, but my mind was a mix of senseless, racing thoughts with scared suicidal considerations. I returned to the doctor in despair, and pleaded with him for help. The doctor changed the medication and increased the dose of both antidepressants and sleeping pills. I started feeling even more sick, and the sensation of the loss of my mother worsened. The pills made me feel sleepy and zombie-like. I tried to continue studying and working, but to be honest, I wasn't productive. The doctor suggested that I take a break. Coincidentally, the university holidays were about to begin.

During my holiday, I literally hibernated; because of the pills, I slept almost all day and night for the entire month. After that, I started feeling a bit better. I slowly returned to my routine. However, birthdays, Christmas and New Year's were the biggest challenges for me. I didn't want to feel sad and make people around me sad too, but that was uncontrollable.

Some months later I got married, and four years later, my first child was born. I felt completely fulfilled as a mother. Eighteen months later my second son was born, bringing even more meaning to my life. I was so happy and, for me, the birth of my second child was the icing on the cake.

I looked at my small family and I felt so proud of myself for having survived the hard times. And then, my first child became ill. He started having lung complications and the doctors were struggling to find a diagnosis. At the time, we had very good private health insurance. The insurance offered him access to the best doctors, hospitals and laboratories in Brazil. He was in and out of the hospital frequently.

After some years of struggle, when he was almost four years old, he was sleeping in the hospital bed connected to the serum receiving medication when the nurse came into our room to check his pulse and his breathing. At that moment, the nurse looked at me with fear on her face. She immediately rang the bell of the doctor's room, and, in seconds, about ten health professionals were hovering over my son. My son wasn't sleeping as I had thought; he was dying. When I saw this scene, I went to the toilet and cried as I had never cried in my entire life. That day, in my despair, I begged God to not take my son away from me, and to my surprise, He listened, and my son survived that ordeal.

Over the past four years, the continuous use of antibiotics to control consecutive episodes of pneumonia had broken down his immune system. After so many times running with him from one doctor to another, one doctor found the diagnosis:

CHAPTER 13: The Gain From the Pain

gastroesophageal reflux. By the time of the diagnosis, the stomach acid had severely damaged my son's insides, and his case was so critical that doctors said that he was just one step away from cancer in his lungs, stomach, oesophagus and pancreas.

The doctor decided to try an emergency surgery and sent us to see the head of the team. At that time, Dr. Sergio Schettini was considered the leading expert in paediatric gastroenterology in Brazil. He said that, in his thirty years of medicine, he had never seen anything even close to my son's case. He looked at my son, at the time burning up with fever, and said, "It is a miracle to see your son alive." He added, "This case is so severe that, even with the surgery, I cannot promise you anything. I am going to try my best." At that moment, I felt like the ground had come out from under me.

A few days later, my son had the surgery and, thank God, the surgery was a success. I saw a miracle happening in our lives. The surgery put an end to our suffering. My son is completely healed. He has never been sick again, not even with a simple flu.

As for my father...for many years, my relationship with him was problematic. I consider myself a non-violent person. I hate disagreements and fighting. My father had the power of making me go from zero to the boiling point in seconds. He knew that and had no mercy; he frequently provoked me, using his power against me. For years, I wasn't able to have a civilized conversation with him. When I understood that his presence was killing me, I avoided him as much as I could in an effort to create a kind of immunity from him. The time and the distance did work and helped with the healing process.

Suddenly, my father took ill and I felt a profound desire to see him. I went to the hospital and saw a man who was old, fragile and sick. I don't know why, but I just felt compassion for him. That day, one thought came to my heart — to become a doctor you need to study for many years. It's the same with any other profession. To be a parent there isn't any preparatory course and you don't need a diploma or a license. I am not a perfect mother...far from it. And I failed to find a perfect father for my sons. If I am not perfect, how can I ask others for perfection? My father was a terrible father and an awful husband, but his behaviour was partially due to my mother's failure lack of action. In that moment, I realized that I had no more space in my heart to keep resentment for him. I truly forgave all the things he had done to me. During his time in the hospital, I did my best to care for him. I felt like all barriers were broken down. Believe me, it was a huge internal transformation for me. After that day, my father's heath got better.

Sometime later, I had another challenging situation in my life. We faced a crippling economic recession in Brazil in 2008. My husband and I had some savings invested in the stock market. Suddenly, all the companies we had invested in had "gone bust" and, in a single day, we lost absolutely everything. All of our money was gone.

In an act of desperation, I left my husband and my sons in Brazil and flew to Europe to work and study in an attempt to get a better life.

One month after I arrived in Portugal, I received a call from my husband saying that my father had suddenly passed away. I cried, but I had peace in my heart, no remorse at all. I think I had won the battle with my depression when I put down all my resentments about him and forgave him. I am very glad I did that before his death, not because he deserved to be forgiven, but because I deserved to be free from the prison of resentment that was in my heart, slowly killing me day by day.

Few months later, I moved again to England, and then new challenges appeared —new language, new culture and cold weather.

CHAPTER 13: The Gain From the Pain

My family came to join me and my older son didn't have any problems adjusting to the new country. Unfortunately, my younger son became a victim of bullying at his new school.

My husband also had problems adapting to the new country. He had always liked spending time and losing himself on the internet. After two years living in England, my husband started showing signs of compulsion and behavioural changes. He started to become aggressive, very irritated, didn't sleep at all because of online gaming addiction. Often, I tried to speak with him and make him aware of the problem, but he didn't listen or wouldn't believe. My marriage got worse and I started feeling the signs of depression again. I was feeling conflicted and I didn't know what to do.

One day I saw my husband very angry, running towards my son, even though my son had done nothing to deserve that reaction. On that day, I tried to speak with him again, but I saw the anger in his eyes and, in that moment, I realised that physical violence against me and my boys was imminent. Though I loved him, I decided to end my eighteen years of marriage. I did that because no child deserves to live in a troubled home, watching and receiving verbal and physical aggression. The behaviour of my husband was at odds with everything I had taught my sons. He was supposed to help me to be a good role model to our children, but unfortunately, that wasn't the case. My ex-husband returned to Brazil, and since so rarely he contact my sons or me again.

I learnt, after 4 years, what it was like to be a single mother in a strange country. I can say that it is a very hard mission. The language barrier made me very vulnerable. I worked hard and studied even harder, because of that, I have had many victories. Last year, I received one more degree in psychology from the University of East London. Now, I am doing a master's degree in Public Health. My older son is also taking a university course, and my younger is an outstanding pupil in the Sixth Form.

My relationship with my sons is perfect. It is more that I could have expected or dreamed. My secret to that is easy; I always was, and continue to be, honest with my sons about my fears and expectations. They suffered a lot at the beginning of my divorce, missing their father's presence because he had gone to live in Brazil. However, they understood my reasons for getting a divorce, and thank God, with time, we overcame the pain together.

I totally agree with the wise words of Greta Gerwig when she says: "I think any breakup from a long relationship has an accompanying feeling of who am I without this person. You feel like a half person because you've integrated yourself into an idea of a couple for so long, and then teasing that out and finding out who you are without them, it just takes a while. It feels like an amputation".

When I look back on my life, I see how hard it was to get here. My faith, optimism and a lot of hard work have been my tools to keep me on the right track and moving forward, no matter what. From the many situations I have encountered, I learnt that with all pain comes the opportunity to grow. Life is worth fighting for, and yes, there is gain behind the pain.

CHAPTER 14

The Power of Love

...One of my friends expects everything of the universe, and is disappointed when anything is less than the best...I begin at the other extreme, expecting nothing, and I am always full of thanks for moderate goods.
~ Ralph Waldo Emerson (1803-1882)

If you feel that the anxiety in your life is out of your control, I have good news for you! You can't control the situation around you, but you can control the way you react to it. Managing anxiety is about assuming responsibility and taking control of your life, including your feelings, emotions, managing your schedule and the way you deal with matters. The management of stress includes changing the upsetting circumstances when you can, altering your response when you can't, protecting yourself and setting aside some time to rest and relax.

Mastering your senses to overcome anxiety is a bit like learning how to drive a car. You can't acquire all the required skills in one lesson; you need to practice until it becomes automatic. When you understand the necessary skills to manage your anxiety, practice them. Doing so will make you feel confident in handling even the hardest of circumstances.

Along with a healthful diet, there are small tips that you can do to feed your soul and confidence, and support your efforts to overcome anxiety, depression and stress.

Stay Socially Engaged

Chat with a receptive friend; talking can increase hormone levels and decrease the severity of your anxiety. It may not change your situation. However, it can help you see things from another perspective and help you find another way to riddle the basis of the problem. Open your heart; sharing your feelings with others isn't a sign of weakness. It is the opposite; it requires control and courage to expose what is upsetting you. Honestly, most people will feel privileged that you trust them enough to share confidential information with them and it will strengthen your bond.

Walking with a friend in the dark is better than walking alone in the light.

~ Helen Keller

Be Trustworthy

Do yourself a favour. Always tell the truth! Start with being honest with yourself and with others. It doesn't matter how hard the truth may be to speak aloud. Wrap the truth in love. Be kind and polite when you express your opinions and feelings. Yes! You can't plant seeds for potatoes and expect them to grow into strawberries. If you hate others lying to you, don't lie to anyone.

If someone has enough courage to ask you a question seriously, then you should be brave enough to answer truthfully.

~ Cameron Milton

Learning How to Say "No"

It is important that you know your limits and stick to them. Both your personal and professional lives are essential. However, handling more than you can manage is sure to trigger stress. Understand that each time you say "yes", when you really want to say "no", you are increasing your cortisone levels (stress hormone). So don't take on more than you can handle.

When you say 'YES' to others, make sure you are not saying 'NO' to yourself.

~ *Paulo Coelho*

Avoid Destructive Relationships

Be honest with yourself when you realise that a person you care about isn't responding and respecting you in the same way. It is because this person doesn't care about your feelings as you deserve. Be realistic, accept it and move on!

The only feeling of real loss is when you love someone more than you love yourself.

~ *Salman Rushdie*

Express Your Feelings

Don't feel shy about saying, "I love you" and "You are important to me." Expressing your feelings for those you love will make you feel better. It applies to your parents, spouse, partner, kids, and so on. Additionally, show appreciation for those who love you, communicating that in words and actions. We never know when it will be the last encounter.

Feeling gratitude and not expressing it is like wrapping a present and not giving it.

~ *William Arthur Ward*

Maintaining Distance from People Who Stress You Out

If there is a person who continually is causing stress in your life, avoid or limit the amount of time you spend with that person or end the relationship.

Don't let the behaviour of others destroy your inner peace.

~ Dalai Lama

Take Control of Your Surroundings

If the news makes you anxious, avoid it. If traffic makes you nervous, avoid rush hour or choose alternative routes. If going out to shop is unpleasant for you, purchase your goods online.

Surround yourself with love. Protect your heart with peace. Live your life in the light.

~ Alex Elle

Watch Your Thoughts

Make an effort to think in a positive way and watch your mouth. Bad thoughts about yourself, dirty words and constant complaining may look like a good way to relieve stress, but it isn't. In fact, there is power in the words. So instead of using words to *recall* bad things and remind yourself about your bad *luck*, use this *power* to say good things, attracting what you want. For each bad thought, think of five good ones.

In optimism there is magic. In pessimism, there is nothing.

~ Abraham-Hicks

Manage Your Time

Poor time management can bring a considerable amount of anxiety. However, when you plan ahead you aren't overextending yourself, and you'll find it easier to stay calm and focused.

CHAPTER 14: The Power of Love

The bad news is time flies. The good news is you're the pilot.
~ Michael Altshuler

Learn from Others' Mistakes

Pay attention to others around you and learn from their mistakes, too. It will teach you a lot and help you to avoid much pain.

Learn from the mistakes of others. You can never live long enough to make them all by yourself.
~ Groucho Marx

Learn to Forgive Others

Accept the fact that we live in an unreliable world and that people make mistakes. Don't give room in your heart to feelings like anger and resentment. Remember that you also make mistakes. Try to live in peace with others by avoiding unnecessary disagreements and fights.

When I forgave those who hurt me, doesn't mean that I accept their behaviour or trust on them. Forgiveness does not change the past, but it does enlarge your future.
~ Paul Boese

Love and Forgive Yourself

You are unique! You were created to become all that you desire to be; you have been predestined to be filled with joy, peace and happiness. Do yourself a favour and allow your inner light full of brilliance to shine out brightly.

The more you like yourself, the less you are like anyone else, which makes you unique.
~ Walt Disney

Enjoy Sex and Intimacy

Sex and romantic intimacy are distinctly different. Sex is simply the act of intercourse, with a physical gratification of enjoyment that ideally ends in orgasm. Romantic intimacy is an emotional connection you share with someone close to your heart. They are not mutually exclusive. That means you can have one without the other. The combination of love and sex requires commitment, a particular type of chemistry that appears between the two and an ability to build intimacy.

Real intimacy is built in stages; it can't be forced or hurried. It tends to follow its own peculiar timeline and trust is a key word here. It needs a continuous attention, I compare relationship intimacy to a crystal glass; it is very easy to break. Unless you trust that you're safe and secure, your intimate interactions will be unsatisfactory.

This combination of time and trust in a relationship is sublime, empowering, and soul enhancing and contributes to your sense of well-being and self-worth. In a trusting relationship, you feel safe, calm and remarkably free. When you have a healthy intimate relationship, you can share your deepest, most profound thoughts without fear of reprisals. If you are having difficulties in your sexual life, talk with your partner. If this doesn't work ask for help. And why not to consider a professional help when it is needed?

The joy of intimacy is the reward of commitment.

~ Kamari Aka Lyrikal

Give Your Time

Offering your time to help others is an awesome way to connect with others and contribute to relieving stress. Research shows that people who help others as volunteering or community work become more resilient and happy.

CHAPTER 14: The Power of Love

Start trying to do someone a favour every day. It can be something as small as helping someone to cross the road. Favours cost nothing to do. Learn that the most precious gift you can offer anyone is your attention.

The meaning of life is to find your gift. The purpose of life is to give it away.

~ Pablo Picasso

Take Time for Yourself

You can reduce stress in your life by nurturing yourself. If you regularly make break time for socialising, relaxation, exercise and fun. Especially those that demand your creativity, and dig your hands in. It can be anything, like playing the piano, painting, gardening, drawing and so on. It is a great therapy for the mind, body and soul.

Giving yourself some loving attention isn't selfish – it's sensible. If you feel loved and cherished (even if it's only by yourself) you'll have more love to give to others.

~ Penelope Quest

Listen to Music

When possible, listen to music aloud and move as much you can. If you have children, invite them to dance together so you have a party. Take dance classes; they are an outstanding way to enhance your wellbeing.

Music touches us emotionally, where words alone can't.

~ Johnny Depp

Be at Peace with Yourself

Don't worry about what others think about you. Their opinions matter only to them. Concentrate your focus and energy on your life and move on.

> *If you cannot find peace within yourself, you will never find it anywhere else.*
>
> ~ *Marvin Gaye*

Keep Your Sense of Humour

This includes the ability to laugh at yourself. Laughing is the best therapy; there is no better anti-aging than this. It helps your body fight oxidative stress in several ways. Try to be around children and animals.

> *I have not seen anyone dying of laughter, but I know millions who are dying because they are not laughing.*
>
> ~*Dr. Madan Kataria*

Educate Yourself

Make education a priority. Read and study always. Continuous learning makes you proactive, emotionally resilient and confident. It empowers you with knowledge, helping you to set goals, challenges and considerably increase the choices you have to achieve your goals. Try learning a new language, a new skill or sport. Your age doesn't matter. It is never too late to start learning a new skill.

> *Formal education will make you a living; self-educating will make you a fortune.*
>
> ~ *Jim Rohn*

Set Goals for the Future

Set clear plans and allow yourself to dream about them. Keep the focus and start working now toward the realisation of your dreams.

> *It always seems impossible until it's done.*
>
> ~ *Nelson Mandela*

Get a Pet

Research has shown that pets provide support to individuals undergoing stressful times. They remind you constantly that you are special and loved.

Having a dog or cat will open your heart. Reading a book will open your mind. Having both a pet and a book is absolute heaven.

~ Mark Rubinstein

Practice a Faith

There are many studies showing that spirituality contributes positively to mental and physical health; they also show that spiritual activity increases wellbeing and resilience and reduces recovery time.

Do you know what is fear? Fear is the absence of love. We were designed by God to freely receive and give love. Unfortunately, when you grow up seeing and receiving the opposite of love you learn to feel fear. For example, a child who grows up in a toxic environment or with a disturbed family model, this child will learn to feel fears and these fears will mould her identity. The negative feelings will be present and engraved in her/ his mind and it will generate shyness, low self-esteem, insecurities, inadequacy, rejection and anxieties in her/ his identity. Somehow, as an adult, the consequences of growing up in that environment will appear and this person will feel lost. When you feel lost in your identity, not knowing your real value and what you are able to do, you also lose your direction and do not know where you are going to and what your mission in the world is.

You might be able to justify the situation you are in right now by pointing the situations you were exposed on the past. However, you can't do anything to change your past. But you can't allow your past to determine who you'll be in the future.

You have free will. This gives you the opportunity to change your thoughts about yourself and change your posture to confront the challenges that come to you. When I understood that in my life, I felt fear, but I chose not to let my fears stop me. I chose to fight to have better days and to leave a legacy. In addition, I found in God all I needed to come out from my past spider web of problems that were holding me up. I transformed my hurts, frustrations and weakness into a fuel that increases my strengths until I achieve my goals. This is a decision I take every day.

I don't know what you lived in your past, but I can affirm that your past doesn't determine who you will be in your future. You are not reading this book by coincidence. If you came from a sick home as well, you have the power to revert the situation and to use your past as an example of an environment that you don't want your children growing up in. You make every effort necessary to achieve your goals. For example, my mother studied only until key stage 2 in the primary school, my father was illiterate and they were expecting me to hate studies as they did. However, I chose to be different, and even on those days when I was full of fear, my thought was, *I'll fight, doesn't matter if I die right now, I will die fighting to have a fulfilled life.* With my attitude, I broke the hereditary curse of my family. I am able to speak three languages, and my sons are already speaking three languages. I did two undergraduate courses in different countries in different languages, and I am completing a Public Health master's degree now.

To change the story of your life you just need to take baby steps in the right direction. Don't look behind, don't look beside yourself. Just look straight ahead and keep going!

If you want a definition of what is love, don't look in a dictionary, but at Calvary.

~ John Stoot

CHAPTER 14: The Power of Love

You are unique! For some people, the principles and recommendations in this book will be quickly absorbed and adopted after a first read. Some will require a bit of discipline to practice the ideas. For others, making these important life-changing habits will require military style discipline!

Find your way and remember that it doesn't matter which category you are, you are worth the sacrifice!

You shall know the truth, and the truth shall make you free.

~John 8:32

Contacting the Author

To contact the author Roseli Schmidt, and share your experiences, your testimonial about the help you received through this book or to have coaching sections with her, please access the website:

www.rswellbeing.com

or email to:

info@rswellbeing.com

You can also follow her on the social media

www.facebook.com/rswellbeing

https://twitter.com/rswellbeing

https://uk.pinterest.com/rswellbeing/

Useful Websites

Here are some useful websites where you can find more information about health services in your country:

Psychological Therapy Services

UK
http://www.nhs.uk/Service-Search/Psychological-therapies
http://www.itsgoodtotalk.org.uk/

US
https://therapists.psychologytoday.com/rms/
http://locator.apa.org/

South Africa
http://www.psychotherapy.co.za/
http://www.therapist-directory.co.za/

Canada
http://www.therapist-directory.co.za/
http://www.cmha.ca/

Australia
http://www.psychology.org.au/FindAPsychologist/
http://www.psychology.org.au/FindAPsychologist/

Naturopathy and Integrative Medicine

UK
http://www.naturaltherapypages.co.uk/
http://www.therapy-directory.org.uk/

US
http://www.naturopathic.org/AF_MemberDirectory.asp?version=2
http://findanaturopath.com/

South Africa
http://naturopathy.org.za/
http://www.integrativemedicine.co.za/

Canada
https://www.cand.ca/
http://www.bcna.ca/

Australia
http://www.australiannaturaltherapistsassociation.com.au/
http://www.anpa.asn.au/

Brain Tumour Research Campaign

Registered charity 295895

Brain tumours affect people of all ages, but they kill more children and young adults than any other cancer, yet only 1% of national cancer research funding goes into brain tumours.

(Brain Tumour Research: "Report on National Research Funding, 2013", p3).

Our vision is to:

- Raising awareness of the urgent need for brain tumour research
- Lead a fundraising campaign to support research into and treatment of brain tumours
- Assist the emergence of a multi-disciplinary Brain Tumour Research Centre of Excellence, based at Imperial College London's Charing Cross Hospital.

Donation can be done by:

Lloyds Charing Cross Branch

Name of Account: WAY AHEAD (BTRC)

Sort Code 30-91-79

Account Number: 00066312

For more information about Wendy and the Brain Tumour Research:

- **Wendy Fulcher** | BTRC Founder, Trustee & Fundraiser
- **Brain Tumour Research Campaign** 12-15 Hanger Green London W5 3EL
- Phone: **+44 (0)20 8601 2402** | Mobile: **07887 732 881** | Web : **www.wayahead-btrc.org**
- Email : **wendy@wayahead-btrc.org**

INDEX

Allergies, 52

Anaemia, 82

Antioxidants, 183, 186

Anxiety, 22, 23, 24, 27, 28, 83, 110, 118, 127, 190

Asthma, 83

Caffeine, 31, 178, 186

Calcium, 81, 83, 84, 184

Cancer, 181, 183, 184, 187

Cholesterol, 52

Depression, 22, 27, 52, 110, 128, 175, 176, 183, 191

Detoxification, 176, 177, 178, 179, 180

Diabetes, 52, 84

Essential Fatty Acids, 93

Essential Minerals, 81

Exercise, vi, 107, 108, 109, 110, 112, 113, 116

Fasting, 47, 48, 50

Fibre, 47, 88

Hypertension, 184

Immune System, 21

Inflammation, 95, 183, 186

Insomnia, 22, 83, 97, 186, 188

Iron, 82, 83

Juice Fast, 48

Melatonin, 102, 188

Milk Thistle, 53

Obesity, 177, 186

Organic Food, 60, 64

Osteoarthritis, 84

Osteoporosis, 84

Overactive Bladder, 105

Pesticides, 58, 180, 181

Potassium, 82, 83

Probiotics, 86, 87, 186

Proteins, 82, 88

Psoriasis, 52, 184, 186

Relaxation, 101, 124, 188

Selenium, 83, 84, 184

Serotonin, 129

Sodium, 82

Sugar, 38

Vitamin A, 67, 84, 183, 184, 187

Vitamin B1, 68, 74, 75, 92

Vitamin B12, 74, 75, 92

Vitamin B2, 69

Vitamin B3, 70

Vitamin B5, 70

Vitamin B6, 71

Vitamin B7, 72

Vitamin B9, 73

Vitamin C, 54, 76, 77, 183, 184, 186

Vitamin D, 77

Vitamin E, 79, 83

Vitamin K, 80, 81

Zinc, 83, 84, 183, 184, 186

BIBLIOGRAPHY

- Anon., n.d. Iz quotes.com. [Online]
  Available at: http://izquotes.com/quote/135288
  [Accessed 29 06 2015].

- Anon., n.d. Trans4mind.com. [Online]
  Available at: http://www.trans4mind.com/counterpoint/index-spiritual/moorehead.shtml
  [Accessed 29 05 2015].

Chapter 1

- Anderson, R., 1998. Cleanse & Purify Thyself. MT. Shasta, CA: Triumph.
  Anon., n.d. Curezone.org. [Online]
  Available at: "Liver Flush". (2015).
  http://www.curezone.org/cleanse/liver.
  [Accessed 08 07 2015].

- Anon., n.d. Ener-chi.com. [Online]
  Available at: http://www.ener-chi.com/history-of-the-liver-and-gallbladder-flush.
  [Accessed 29 08 2015].

- Anon., n.d. Guardianlv.com. [Online]
  Available at: http://guardianlv.com/2013/10/water-ionizers-can- cause-more-harm-than-good-video.
  [Accessed 12 09 2015].

- Anon., n.d. Niddk.nih.gove. [Online]
  Available at: http://www.niddk.nih.gov/health-information/health-topics/digestive-diseases/gallstones/Pages/facts.aspx
  [Accessed 12 07 2015].

- Anon., n.d. Retrieved from Gogood Reads.com. [Online]
  Available at: Retrhttp://www.goodreads.com/quotes/3097-there-is-an-indian-proverb-that-says-that-e
  [Accessed 27 05 2015].

- Caspi, A., et al., 2003. Influence of Life Stress on Depression: Moderation by a Polymorphism in the 5-HTT Gene I. Science, Volume 386, pp. 301.

- Calbom, C., 2008. The Lady's Guide To Juicing For Health: A Practical A-to-Z Guide To The Prevention And Treatment of Most Common Health Disorders. England: Penguin Group.

- Chalford, G., n.d. Understanding the Healing Crisis. Upwardquest.com. [Online]
  Available at: Retrieved from http://www.upwardquest.com/healing-crisis.html.
  [Accessed 20 06 2015].

BIBLIOGRAPHY

- Csikszentmihalyi, M., 1990. Flow: The Psychology of Optimal Experience. New York: Harper & Row.
- Page, L., 1999. Detoxification. Camel Valley, CA: Healthy Healing Publication.

Chapter 2

- Anon., n.d. Adaa.org. [Online]
  Available at: http://www.adaa.org/understanding-anxiety
  [Accessed 29 08 2015].
- Anderson, R., 1998. Cleanse & Purify Thyself. MT. Shasta, CA: Triumph.
  Anon., n.d. Curezone.org. [Online]
  Available at: "Liver Flush". (2015).
  http://www.curezone.org/cleanse/liver.
  [Accessed 08 07 2015].
- Anon., n.d. Ener-chi.com. [Online]
  Available at: http://www.ener-chi.com/history-of-the-liver-and-gallbladder-flush/
  [Accessed 29 08 2015].
- Anon., n.d. Guardianlv.com. [Online]
  Available at: http://guardianlv.com/2013/10/water-ionizers-can- cause-more-harm-than-good-video/
  [Accessed 12 09 2015].
- Anon., n.d. Niddk.nih.gov. [Online]
  Available at: http://www.niddk.nih.gov/health-information/health-topics/digestive-diseases/gallstones/Pages/facts.aspx
  [Accessed 12 07 2015].
- Anon., n.d. Retrieved from Go Good Reads.com. [Online]
  Available at: (2005, 05 27).
  Retrhttp://www.goodreads.com/quotes/3097-there-is-an-indian-proverb-that-says-that-e
  [Accessed 27 05 2015].
- Anon., n.d. Retrieved from Smart Recovery.org. [Online]
  Available at: (2005, 05 27). Retrhttp://www.smartrecovery.org
  [Accessed 27 05 2015].
- Calbom, C., 2008. The Lady's Guide To Juicing For Health: A Practical A-to-Z Guide To The Prevention And Treatment of Most Common Health Disorders. England: Penguin Group.
- Caspi, A., et al., 2003. Influence of Life Stress on Depression: Moderation by a Polymorphism in the 5-HTT Gene I. Science, Volume 386, pp. 301.
- Chalford, G., n.d. Understanding the Healing Crisis. Upwardquest.com. [Online]
  Available at: Retrieved from http://www.Upwardquest.com/healing-crisis.html.
  [Accessed 20 06 2015].
- Courtois, C. A. & Ford, J. D, 2009. Treating Complex Traumatic Stress Disorders: An Evidence-Based Guide. New York: The Guilford Press.

- Hagnell O, Lanke J, Rorsman B, Jesjo L., 1982. Are we entering an age of melancholy ? Depressive illnesses in a prospective epidemiological study over 25 years: The Lundby study, Sweden. Psychological Medicine Volume 12,pp. 279–289.
- Page, L., 1999. Detoxification. Camel Valley, CA: Healthy Healing Publication.

Chapter 3

- Anon., n.d. Iluv Quotes.com. [Online]
  Available at: http://iluvquotes.com/sensitive-people-suffer-love-dream-augusto-cury/
  [Accessed 05 06 2015].
- Anderson, R., 1998. Cleanse & Purify Thyself. MT. Shasta, CA: Triumph.
- Anon., n.d. Curezone.org. [Online]
  Available at: "Liver Flush". (2015).
  http://www.curezone.org/cleanse/liver.
  [Accessed 08 07 2015].
- Anon., n.d. Ener-Chi.com. [Online]
  Available at: http://www.ener-chi.com/history-of-the-liver-and-gallbladder-flush/
  [Accessed 29 08 2015].
- Anon., n.d. Guardianlv.com. [Online]
  Available at: http://guardianlv.com/2013/10/water-ionizers-can- cause-more-harm-than-good-video/
  [Accessed 12 09 2015].
- Anon., n.d. Niddk.nih.gove. [Online]
  Available at: http://www.niddk.nih.gov/health-information/health-topics/digestive-diseases/gallstones/Pages/facts.aspx
  [Accessed 12 07 2015].
- Anon., n.d. Retrieved from Go Good Reads.com. [Online]
  Available at: (2005, 05 27).
  Retrhttp://www.goodreads.com/quotes/3097-there-is-an-indian-proverb-that-says-that-e
  [Accessed 27 05 2015].
- Calbom, C., 2008. The Lady's Guide To Juicing For Health: A Practical A-to-Z Guide To The Prevention And Treatment of Most Common Health Disorders. England: Penguin Group.
  Chalford, G., n.d. Understanding the Healing Crisis. Upwardquest.com. [Online]
  Available at: Retrieved from http://www.upwardquest.com/healing-crisis.html.
  [Accessed 20 06 2015].
- Clementz, G. L., & Dailey, J.W., 1988. Psychotropic Effects of Caffeine. American Family Physician. Volume 37, pp. 167-172.
- D' Astrous, A., 1990. An Inquiry Into the Compulsive Side of Normal Consumers. Journal of Consumer policy, 15-31.

BIBLIOGRAPHY

- Faith, M. S., 1997. Emotional Eating and Obesity: Theoretical Considerations and Practical Recommendations: Overweight and Weight management: The Health Professional's Guide to Understand and Practice. Gaithersburg: Aspen Publishers.
- Keers, R., 2012. Gene-environment Interaction in Major Depression and Antidepressant Treatment Response. Curr Psychiatry Rep. Volume 14(2), pp. 129-37.
- Lane, J D; Adcock, R A; Williams, R B; Kuhn, C M. 1990. Caffeine Effects on Cardiovascular and Neuroendocrine Responses to Acute Psychosocial Stress and Their Relationship to Level of Habitual Caffeine Consumption. Psychosomatic Medicine. Volume 52(3), pp. 247-367.
- Page, L., 1999. Detoxification. Camel Valley, CA: Healthy Healing Publication.
- Van Den Berg, A. E., Hartig, T., Staats, H. 2007. Preference for Nature in Urbanized Societies: Stress, Restoration, and the Pursuit of Sustainability. Journal of Social Issues
- Volume 63 (1), pp. 79–96.

Chapter 4

- Anderson, R., 1998. Cleanse & Purify Thyself. MT. Shasta, CA: Triumph.
- Anon., n.d. Curezone.org. [Online]
  Available at: Liver Flush. (2015). http://www.curezone.org/cleanse/liver.
  [Accessed 08 07 2015].
- Anon., n.d. Ener-chi.com. [Online]
  Available at: http://www.ener-chi.com/history-of-the-liver-and-gallbladder-flush/
  [Accessed 29 08 2015].
- Anon., n.d. Guardianlv.com. [Online]
  Available at: http://guardianlv.com/2013/10/water-ionizers-can- cause-more-harm-than-good-video/
  [Accessed 12 09 2015].
- Anon., n.d. Niddk.nih.gove. [Online]
  Available at: http://www.niddk.nih.gov/health-information/health-topics/digestive-diseases/gallstones/Pages/facts.aspx
  [Accessed 12 07 2015].
- Anon., n.d. Retrieved from Go Good Reads.com. [Online]
  Available at: (2005, 05 27).
  Retrhttp://www.goodreads.com/quotes/3097-there-is-an-indian-proverb-that-says-that-e
  [Accessed 27 05 2015].
- Anon., n.d. Retrieved who.int. [Online]
  Available at: (2005, 05 27).
  Retrhttp://www.who.int/water_sanitation_health/publications/2011/ph armaceuticals_20110601.pdf
  [Accessed 27 05 2015].

- Cal, K., 2006. Skin Penetration of Terpenes From Essential Oils And Topical Vehicles. Planta Med. 2006 Volume 72(4). pp. 311-6.
- Calbom, C., 2008. The Lady's Guide to Juicing For Health: A Practical A-to-Z Guide To The Prevention And Treatment of Most Common Health Disorders. England: Penguin Group.
- Chalford, G., n.d. Understanding the Healing Crisis. Upwardquest.com. [Online]
  Available at: Retrieved from http://www.upwardquest.com/healing-crisis.html.
  [Accessed 20 06 2015].
- Candance, P., 1997. Molecules of Emotions: Why You Feel The Way You Fell. New York: Scribner.
- Cannon, G. 2002. Nutrition: The New world Disorder. Asia Pacific Journal Clin. Nutri Volume 11, Suppl 3, S498-509.
- Connor, E. b., 1997. Metal and Oxidative Damage in Neurological Disorders. Pennsylvania: Plenum Press.
- Forster, M. B., 2009. "Topical Delivery of Cosmetics and Drugs. Molecular Aspects of Percutaneous Absorption and Delivery". Eur J. Dermatol, 309-323.
- Herman, S. L., 2012. Electrical Transformers and Rotating Machines. New York: Delmar Cengage Learning.
- Page, L., 1999. Detoxification. Camel Valley, CA: Healthy Healing Publication.
- Peterson, D. T., 2010. Reproductive Endocrinology and Infertility: Integrating Modern Clinical and Laboratory Practice. New York: Springer.
- Yang, C.S., G. Lu, and G.X. Li., 2010. Inhibition of inflammation and carcinogenesis in the lung and colon by tocopherols. Ann N.Y. Acad Sci Volume 1203. Pp.29-34.

Chapter 5

- Anderson, R., 1998. Cleanse & Purify Thyself. MT. Shasta, CA: Triumph.
- Anon., n.d. Curezone.org. [Online]
  Available at: Curezone "Liver Flush". (2015).
  http://www.curezone.org/cleanse/liver.
  [Accessed 08 07 2015].
- Anon., n.d. Ener-chi.com. [Online]
  Available at: http://www.ener-chi.com/history-of-the-liver-and-gallbladder-flush.
  [Accessed 29 08 2015].
- Anon., n.d. Guardianlv.com. [Online]
  Available at: http://guardianlv.com/2013/10/water-ionizers-can- cause-more-harm-than-good-video.
  [Accessed 12 09 2015].
- Anon., n.d. Niddk.nih.gove. [Online]

BIBLIOGRAPHY

- Available at: http://www.niddk.nih.gov/health-information/health-topics/digestive-diseases/gallstones/Pages/facts.aspx
  [Accessed 12 07 2015].
- Anon., n.d. Retrieved from Go Good Reads.com. [Online]
  Available at: (2005, 05 27).
  Retrhttp://www.goodreads.com/quotes/3097-there-is-an-indian-proverb-that-says-that-e
  [Accessed 27 05 2015].
- Calbom, C., 2008. The Lady's Guide To Juicing For Health: A Practical A-to-Z Guide To The Prevention And Treatment of Most Common Health Disorders. England: Penguin Group.
- Chalford, G., n.d. Understanding the Healing Crisis. Upwardquest.com. [Online]
  Available at: Retrieved from http://www.upwardquest.com/healing-crisis.html.
  [Accessed 20 06 2015].
- Colbert, D., 2007. The Seven Pillars of Health. Florida. Siloam.
- Moritz, A., 1998. The Amazing Liver Cleanse: A Powerful Approach To Improve Your Health And Vitality. Kindle Edition.
- Morley, C., 2001. Detox: 100 Natural Ways to Cleanse and Purify. Publisher: MQ Publications Ltd
- Page, L., 1999. Detoxification. Camel Valley, CA: Healthy Healing Publication.
- Schwalfenberg, G. k. 2012. The Alkaline Diet: Is There Evidence That an Alkaline pH Diet Benefits Health? Journal of Environmental and Public Health. Volume 2012. Pp 7.

Chapter 6

- Anon., NYCAP Alternatives to Pesticides". Health Effects of Pesticides. [Online]
  Available at:
  http://www.pesticideresearch.com/site/docs/alternatives.pdf.
  [Accessed 28 05 2015].
- Anon., 2000. Banned Pesticides, Others Found on Washington State Apples". (2000). [Online]
  Available at: Banned Pesticides, Others Found on Washington State Apples". (2http://www.ewg.org/banned-pesticide-others-found-was
  [Accessed 23 07 2015].
- Anon., n.d. ewg.org. [Online]
  Available at: Banned Pesticides, Others Found on Washington State Apples (2000).
  http://www.ewg.org/banned-pesticide-others-found-was
  [Accessed 12 08 2015].
- Anon., n.d. Fao.org. [Online]
  Available at: http://www.fao.org/organicag/oa-faq/oa-faq6/en/
  [Accessed 20 09 2015].

- Anon., n.d. Gov.uk. [Online]
  Available at: http://www.gov.uk/guidance/organic-certification-and-standards
  [Accessed 28 10 2015].

- Anon., n.d. Ion.ac.uk. [Online]
  Available at: Soil mineral Depletion:
  http://www.ion.ac.uk/information/onarchives/soilmineraldepletion
  [Accessed 07 07 2015].

- Anon., n.d. Pesticide Action Network. UK.org. [Online]
  Available at http://www.pan-uk.org/
  [Accessed 12 07 2015].

- Anon., n.d. Pesticideresearch.com. [Online]
  Available at: NYCAP Alternatives to Pesticides. Health Effects of Pesticides(19960
  http: www.pesticideresearch.com/site/docs/alternatives.pdf
  [Accessed 12 07 2015].

- Anon., n.d. Roda leinstitute.org. [Online]
  Available at: http://rodaleinstitute.org/assets/FSTbooklet.pdf
  [Accessed 23 10 2015].

- Anon., n.d. Science direct.com. [Online]
  Available at: http://www.sciencedirect.com/science/journal/03778401
  [Accessed 23 09 2015].

- Anon., n.d. The Rx Diaries. (2015). [Online]
  Available at: http://therxdiaries.com/every-time-you-eat-or-drink-you-are-either-feeding-disea.
  [Accessed 09 07 2015].

- Anon., n.d. Usda.gov. [Online]
  Available at: http://www.usda.gov/organic-agriculture.html
  [Accessed 12 06 2015].

- Calbom, C., 2008. The Lady's Guide To Juicing For Health: A Practical A-to-Z Guide To The Prevention And Treatment of Most Common Health Disorders. England: Penguin Group.

- Curl, C. L., 2002. Organophosphorus Pesticides Exposure of Urban and Suburban Pre-School Children with Organic and Conventional Diet. [Online]
  Available at: www.nrdc.org

- Framklin, H., 2001. Beyond Toxicity: Human Health and the Environment. Am J. Prev. Med, Volume 20(3), pp. 234-240.

- Havasi, P., 2012. Education of Cancer Healing. Kindle Edition. Vol VIII-p.208. ed. s.l.:s.n.

- Henneron, L. B., 2015. Fourteen Years of Evidence for Positive Effects of Conservation Agriculture and organic Farming on the Soil Life. Agronomy for Sustainable Development, Volume 35(1), pp. 169-181.

- Horrobin, D., 2003. "Why Do We Not Take More Medical Use of Nutritional Knowledge? How and Inadvertent Alliance Between Reductionist Scientist. "Holistic Dietitians and Drug Oriented Regulators

BIBLIOGRAPHY

and Governments. Br J. Nutr, Volume 90 (1), pp. 233-238.
Nestle, M., 2002. Food Politics: How the food Industry Influences Nutrition and Health. Berkley and Los Angeles: University of California Press, Ltd.

- Pokharel, R. Z., 2015. Impact of Organic and Conventional Peach and Apple. Production Practices on Soil Microbial Populations and Plant Nutrients. Organic Agriculture, Volume 6(1), pp. 19-30.

Chapter 7

- Anon., 2015. Merck Manual Online. [Online]
  Available at: http://www.merck.com/pubs/mmanual/section1/chapter3/3e.htm.
  [Accessed 10 10 2015].

- Anon., n.d. Fda.gov. [Online]
  Available at: http://www.fda.gov/food/GuidanceRegulation/GuidanceDocuments Regulatoryinformation/LabelingNutrition/ucm064928.htm
  [Accessed 23 08 2015].

- Anon., n.d. Fni.nal.usda.gov. [Online]
  Available at: http:/fnic.nal.usda.gov/food-composition/vitamins-and-minerals
  [Accessed 24 09 2015].

- Anon., n.d. Food.gov.uk. [Online]
  Available at: http://food.gov.uk/sites/default/files/multimedia/pdfs/nutrientinstitution.pdf
  [Accessed 23 08 2015].

- Anon., n.d. Health Aliciousness.com. [Online]
  Available at: http://www.healthaliciousness.com/articles/Top-5-Natural-Vegetarian-sources-Vitamin-B12
  [Accessed 01 09 2015].

- Anon., n.d. Heath harvard.edu. [Online]
  Available at: http://www.health.harvard.edu/blog/benefits-vitamin-d-supplements-still-debated-201404047106
  [Accessed 24 08 2015].

- Anon., n.d. Heath harvard.edu. [Online]
  Available at: http://www.health.harvard.edu/staying-healthy/listing_of_vitamins
  [Accessed 24 08 2015].

- Anon., n.d. http://yournewvitality.com/easyblog/entry/what-you-don-t-eat-will-kill-you. [Online]
  Available at: http://yournewvitality.com/easyblog/entry/what-you-don-t-eat-will-kill-you
  [Accessed 29 07 2015].

- Anon., n.d. NHS.UK. [Online]
  Available at: http://www.nhs.uk/vitamins
  [Accessed 22 09 2015].

- Anon., n.d. Nimh.nih.gov. [Online]
  Available at: http://www.nimh.nih.gov/health/topics/depression/index.shtml
  [Accessed 24 09 2015].

- Anon., n.d. Odss.od.nih.gov. [Online]
  Available at: http://odss.od.nih.gov/factsheets/Zinc-Healthprofessional.
  [Accessed 10 09 2015].

- Anon., n.d. Shape.com. [Online]
  Available at: Retrieved from Shape.com: http://www.shape.com/healthy-eating/diet-tips/smartest-things-ever-said-about-dieting/slide/7
  [Accessed 23 07 2015].

- Basu, S. S., 2003. Single Megadose Vitamin A Supplementation of Indian Mothers and Morbidity in Breastfed Young Infants. Postgrad. Med. Journal, Volume 79(933), pp. 397-402.

- Calbom, B. C., 2006. "The Complete Cancer Cleanse: A Proven Program to Detoxity and Renew Body, Mind, and Spirit. Tennessee: Thomas Nelson.

- Chandra, R. K., 1994. Zinc and Immunition. Nutrition, 10(1), pp. 79-80.

- Colbin, A., 1986. Food and Healing. New York: Ballantine Books.

- Denko, C. W., 1981. Inflammation in Relation to Dietary Intake of Zinc and Copper. International Journal of Tissue recreations, Volume 3, pp. 73-76.

- Emerging Evidence, P., 2004. Geneva, Switzerland: World Health Organization: [Online]
  Available at: http://www.who.int/mentalhealth/evidence/en/promotingmhh.pdf

- European Food Safety Authority, S. C. o. F. (. R. f. E. h.., 2006. European Food Safety Authority, Scientific Committee on Food. Efsa.europa.eu. [Online]
  Available at: http://efsa.europa.eu/sites/default/files/efsa_rep/.../ndatolerableuil.pdf
  [Accessed 20 07 2015].

- Farrow, L. B., 2013. The Iodine Crisis: What You Don't Know About Iodine Can Wreck Your Life". Kindle Edition ed. S. L: Lyne Farrow..

- Grimble, R. F., 1994. Nutrition Antioxidants and the Modulation of Inflammation: Theory and Practice. Institute of Human Nutrition, University of Southampton, UK, 2(2), pp. 175-185.

- Haas, E. M., 1992. Staying Healthy with Nutrition. Berkeley, CA: Celestial Arts.

- Halpern, G. M., 1993. Nutrition and Immunity: Where Are We Standing? Allergy and Immunophathology, 21(3), pp. 122-126.

- Hoffer, A. S., 2008. Orthomolecular Medicine for Everyone: Megavitamins Therapeutics for families and Physicians. CA: Basic Health Publications, Inc.

- Jonson, B. H., 2012. The Vitamin Cure: For Depression. Canada: Basic

BIBLIOGRAPHY

Health.

- Mahan, K. L.-S., 1996. krause's Food, Nutrition and Diet Therapy. 9th ed. Philadelphia: W.B. Saunders.
- Mindell, E. M., 2004. Vitamin Bible. New York: Time Warner Book Group.
- Murray, F., 1990. "Nutrient Therapy Relieves Skin Ailments; B-Complex Vitamins, Omega-3 Fish Oils, Vitamin C and Zinc Help Alleviate Psoriasis and Eczema. [Online]
  Available at: http://findarticle.com/p/articles/mi_mo860/is_n4_v52/ai_883050p
  [Accessed 09 08 2015].
- Omennal, G. S. (1996). Effects of a Combination of Beta Carotene and Vitamin A on Lung Cancer and Cardiovascular Disease. *New England Journal of Medicine*, 334:1150-1155.
- Pauling, L., 1976. Vitamin C. The common Cold and Flu. San Francisco: W.H. Freeman & Company.
- Pitchford, P., 1993. Healing With Whole Foods: Oriental Traditions and Modern Nutrition. Berkeley, CA: North Atlantic Books.
- Porter, J. M., 1981. Bed-Time Food Supplements and Sleep: Effects of Different Carbohydrate Levels.". Electroencephalography and Clinical Neurophysiology, Volume 51, pp. 426-433.
- Rahmathullah, T. L., 2003. Impact of Supplementing Newborn Infants with Vitamin A on Early Infant Mortality: Community-based Randomized Trial in Sothern India. Br Med Journal, Volume 327:7409, pp. 254.
- Regland, B. E., 1995. Homocysteine is a common feature of Schizophrenia. J. Neural Transm Gen Sect, 100(2), pp. 165-169.
- Rosanoff, A., 2005. Magnesium and Hypertension. Clinical Calcium, 15(2), pp. 255-260.
- Shauzer, G. N., 1992. Selenium and the Immune Response. The Nutritional Report, 10(3), pp. 17,24.
- Silverman, H. M., 1999. The Vitamin Book. Canada: Bantam Books.
- Solzback, U. E., 1997. Vitamin C Improves Endothelial Dysfunction of Epicardial Coronary Arteries in Hypertensive Patients. Circulation, 96(5), pp. 1513-1519.
- Swain, R. E., 1995. Vitamins as Therapy in the 1990's. Journal of the American Board of Family Practice, Volume 8, pp. 206.
- Victor, M. A., 1961. On The Aetiology of the Alcoholic Neurologic Diseases With Special Reference to the Role of Nutrition. Am. J. Clin. Nutr. Volume 9, pp. 379-397.
- Wan, J. M., 1989. Nutrition, Immune Function, and inflammation: An Overview. Proceedings of the Nutrition Society, Volume 48, pp. 315-335.

Chapter 8

- Anon., n.d. Whfoods.com. [Online]
  Available at: www.whfoods.com/genpage.php?tname=nutrient&dbid=119
  [Accessed 10 07 2015].

- Anon., n.d. Bbc.co.uk. [Online]
  Available at: http://www.bbc.co.uk/news/health-34615621
  [Accessed 10 10 2015].

- Anon., n.d. Fda.gov: [Online]
  Available at:
  http://www.fda.gov/food/GuidanceRegulation/GuidanceDocuments
  Regulatoryinformation/LabelingNutrition/ucm064928.htm
  [Accessed 23 08 2015].

- Anon., n.d. Ion.ac.uk. [Online]
  Available at:
  http://www.ion.ac.uk/information/onarchives/soilmineraldepletion
  [Accessed 30 08 2015].

- Anon., n.d. Labmed.ucsf.edu. [Online]
  Available at: http://www.labmed.ucsf.edu/labmanual/mftlng-mtzn/test/refreange.html.
  [Accessed 09 09 2015].

- Anon., n.d. Lifeextension.com. [Online]
  Available at: http://lifeextension.com/protocols/appendix/blood-testing
  [Accessed 27 09 2015].

- Anon., n.d. Livestrong.com. [Online]
  Available at: livestrong.com/article/73159-list-foods-flavonoids
  [Accessed 15 09 2015].

- Anon., n.d. Omega-3.com. [Online]
  Available at: www.omega-3.com/about-omega-3/recommended-intake.
  [Accessed 19 09 2015].

- Anon., n.d. Pinrest.com. [Online]
  Available at: https://www.pinterest.com/pin/438115869972420456.
  [Accessed 01 09 2015].

- Braverman, E. R., 2003. The Healing Nutrients Within: Facts, Finding, and New Research on Amino Acids. Laguna Beach, CA: Basic health Publications-Inc.

- Calbom, C., 2008. "The Lady's Guide To Juicing for Health: A Practical A-to-Z Guide to the Prevention and Treatment of the Most Common Health Disorders". England: Pinguin Group.

- Candance, P., 1997. Molecules of Emotions: Why You Feel The Way You Fell. New York: Scribner.

- Cannon, G., 2002. Nutrition: The New World Disorder. Asia Pacific Journal Clin. Nutri 11 Suppl 3, S498-509.

- Connor, E. b., 1997. Metal and Oxidative Damage in Neurological Disorders. Pennsylvania: Plenum Press.

- Curl, C. L., 2002. Organophosphorus Pesticide Exposure of Urban and

BIBLIOGRAPHY

- Suburban Pre-School Children with Organic and Conventional Diet. www.nrdc.org: Natural Resources defence Council.

- D' Astrous, A., 1990. "An Inquiry Into the Compulsive Side of Normal Consumers." Journal of Consumer Policy, 15-31.

- Denko, C. W., 1981. Inflammation in Relation to Dietary Intake of Zinc and Copper. International Journal of Tissue Recreations, Volume 3, pp. 73-76.

- Espie, C. (2010). "Overcoming Insomnia: A self-help guide using Cognitive Behavioural Techniques. London: Robinson.

- Faith, M. S. (1997). "Emotional Eating and Obesity: Theoretical Considerations and Practical Recommendations": Overweight and Weight Management: The Health Professional's Guide to Understand and Practice. Gaithersburg: Aspen Publishers.

- Forster, M. B. (2009). "Topical Delivery of Cosmetics and Drugs. Molecular Aspects of Percutaneous Absorption and Delivery". Eur J. Dermatol, 309-323.

- Grimble, R. F., 1994. Nutrition Antioxidants and the Modulation of Inflammation: Theory and Practice. Institute of Human Nutrition, University of Southampton, UK, 2(2), pp. 175-185.

- Haas, E. M., 1992. Staying Healthy with Nutrition. Berkeley, CA: Celestial Arts.
Hho.int, (. R. f. h., n.d. who.int. [Online]
Available at: http://who.int/mediacentre/factsheets.
[Accessed 07 06 2015].

- Henneron, L. e. (2002). Organophoshorus Pesticide Exposure of Urban and Suburban Pre-School Children with Organic and Conventional Diet. www.nrdc.org: Natural Resource Defence Council.

- Herman, S. L. (2012). Electrical Transformers and Rotating Machines. New York: Delmar Cengage Learning.

- Huffnagle, G. W. S., 2008. The Probiotics Revolution: The Definitive Guide to Safe, Natural Health Solutions Using Probiotic Foods and Supplements. USA: Bantam Books.

- Johnson, R., 2013. Fermenting Milk Kefir. Vol 3. Kindle Edition. ed. s.l.:s.n.

- Lamberg, L. (2007). "Several Sleep Disorders Reflect Gender Differences". Psychiatric News 42, 40.

- Lane, J. D. (1990). "Caffeine Effects on Cardiovascular and Neuroendocrine Response to Acute Psychosocial Stress and Their Relationship to Level of Habitual Caffeine Consumption". Psychosomatic Medicine 52(3), 320-26.

- Murray, F., 1990. "Nutrient Therapy Relieves Skin Ailments; B-Complex Vitamins, Omega-3 Fish Oils, Vitamin C and Zinc Help Alleviate Psoriasis and Eczema. [Online]
Available at:
http://findarticle.com/p/articles/mi_mo860/is_n4_v52/ai_883050p
[Accessed 09 08 2015].

- Nasjikal. 2015. China Air Quality Monitoring. Google Play. https://play.google.com/store/apps/details?id=com.cas.airquality

- Nestle, M., 2002. Food Politics: How the Food Industry Influences Nutrition and Health. Berkley and Los Angeles: University of California Press, Ltd.

- Omennal, G. S., 1996. Effects of a Combination of Beta Carotene and Vitamin A on Lung Cancer and Cardiovascular Disease. New England Journal of Medicine, 334:1150-1155.

- Peterson, D. T., 2010. Reproductive Endocrinology and Infertility: Integrating Modern Clinical and Laboratory Practice. New York: Springer.

- Pokharel, R. Z., 2015. Impact of Organic and Conventional Peach and Apple Production Practices on Soil Microbial Populations and Plant Nutrients. http://link.springer.com/article/10.1007/s13165-015-0106-6: Organic Agriculture.

- Ribeiro, S. A., 2004. Reverberation, Storage, and Postsynaptic Propagation of Memories During Sleep. Learn Men. 11(6), 686-696.

- Sahley, B. J., 2015. Heal with Amino Acids and Nutrients: A Self-Help Guide for Common Health

- Problems Using Amino Acids and Nutrients. Texas: Pain & stress Publications.

- Wan, J. M., 1989. Nutrition, Immune Function, and inflammation: An Overview. Proceedings of the Nutrition Society, Volume 48, pp. 315-335.

- Sheldon, H., 1988. Body's Introduction to the Study of Disease. Philadelphia: Lea and Scribner.

- Welch, A. S. S., 2010. Dietary Intake And Status Of N-3 Polyunsaturated Fatty Acids In A Population Of Fish-Eating And Non-Fish-Eating Meat-Eaters, Vegetarians, And Vegans And The Product-Precursor Ratio [corrected] Of Alpha-Linolenic Acid To Long-Chain N-3 Polyunsatuted Fatty. Am J Clin Nutr, 92:1040-51.

Chapter 9

- Anon., n.d. *Adrenal Fatigue.org.* [Online]
  Available at: Adrenal Fatigue.org: http://adrenalfatigue.org/what-is-adrenal-fatigue
  [Accessed 21 11 2015].

- Anon., n.d. *Biopsychology.com:.* [Online]
  Available at: http://www.biopsychology.com/news
  [Accessed 12 10 2015].

- Anon., n.d. *Drowsy Driving.org.* [Online]
  Available at: http://drowsydriving.org/about/facts-and-stats
  [Accessed 12 10 2015].

- Anon., n.d. *Drugabuse.gov.* [Online]
  Available at: http://drugabuse.gov/publications/drugfacts/precription-over-counter-medications
  [Accessed 12 10 2015].

BIBLIOGRAPHY

- Anon., n.d. *Erowid.org:.* [Online]
  Available at: http://www.erowid.org/experiences
  [Accessed 09 10 2015].

- Anon., n.d. *Good Reads.com.* [Online]
  Available at: https://www.goodreads.com/author_blog_posts/8111977-the-hours-between-12am-and-6am-have-a-funny-habit-of-making-you-feel-li
  [Accessed 12 10 2015].

- Anon., n.d. *Mental Health.org.uk:.* [Online]
  Available at: http://www.mentalhealth.org.uk/help-information/mental-health-a-z/S/sleep-disorders/
  [Accessed 02 10 2015].

- Anon., n.d. *Nhtsa.gov.* [Online]
  Available at: http://www.nhtsa.gov/
  [Accessed 12 11 2015].

- Anon., n.d. *Nhlbi.nih.gov.* [Online]
  Available at: http://www.nhlbi.nih.gov/health/health-topics/topics/sdd/howmuch
  [Accessed 12 10 2015].

- Anon., n.d. *Sleepio.com.* [Online]
  Available at: http:// "http://www.sleepio.com" www.sleepio.com
  [Accessed 02 11 2015].

- Anon., n.d. *The Guardian.com:* [Online]
  Available at: http://www.theguardian.com/lifeandstyle/2012/sep/22/dreamland-insomnia-sleep-cbt-drugs
  [Accessed 12 11 2015].

- Anon., n.d. *Webmd.com.* [Online]
  Available at: http://www.webmd.com/urinary-incontinence-oab/features/putting-an-overactive-bladder-to-bed
  [Accessed 21 08 2015].

- Berry, E. M., 1987. Foods and Their Effects on Sleep Patterns. *International Clinical Nutrition,* Volume 7, pp. 76-78.

- Challem, J., 2011. *The Complete Nutrition and Lifestyle Program, No more fatigue: Why You're So Tired and What You Can Do About it.* New Jersey: John Wiley & Sons, Inc..

- Comperatore, C. E., 1996. Melatonin Efficacy in Aviation Missions Requiring Rapid Deployment and Night Operations. *Aviation, Space and Environmental Medicine,* 67(6), pp. 520-524.

- Espie, C., 2010. "Overcoming Insomnia: A self-help guide using Cognitive Behavioural Techniques. London: Robinson.

- Friedman, L. B., 1988. A Preliminary Study Comparing Sleep Restriction and Relaxation Treatments for Insomnia in Older Adults. *Oxford Journal-Gerontology Medicine & Health,* p. 46.

- Hartmann, E., 1982. Effects of L-Tryptophan on Sleepiness and on Sleep. *J. Psychiatric Research,* 17(2), pp. 107-113.

- He, Y. J., 2009. The Transcriptional Repressor DEC2Regulates Sleep Lenghth in Mammals. *Science,* 14 (325(5942)), pp. 866-870.

- Lamberg, L., 2007. "Several Sleep Disorders Reflect Gender Differences". *Psychiatric News 42* , 40.

- Loprinzi, P., 2011. Association Between Objectively-Measured Physical Activity and Sleep. *Mental and Physical Activity,* 4(2), pp. 65-69.

- Porter, J. M., 1981. Bed-Time Food Supplements and Sleep: Effects of Different Carbohydrate Levels. *Eletroencephalography and Clinical Neurophysiology,* Volume 51, pp. 426-433.

- Ribeiro, S., Nicolelis, M. A. L., 2004. Reverberation, Storage, And Postsynaptic Propagation Of Memories During Sleep. Learn Mem. 2004, Volume 11(6), pp.686–696.

- Roth, T.; Krystal, A. D. & Lieberman, J. A. 2007. Long-term issues in the treatment of sleep disorders. CNS Spectrums. Volume 127 (Suppl 10), pp. 1–14.

- Stewart W. F., et al (2003) Prevalence And Burden Of Overactive Bladder In The United States (NOBLE Study). World Journal Of Urology; 20, Pp 327-336.

- Strohecker, J., 1994. *The Burton Golberg Group" Alternative Medicine: The Definitive Guide.* Puyallup, WA: Future Medicine Publishing.

- Van Kerrebroek, P., Kreder, K., Jonas, U., Zimmer, N., Wein, A., 2001. Tolteridone Study Group, Tolteridone Once Daily: Superior Efficacy And Tolerability In The Treatment Of The Overactive Bladder. Urology. Volume 57(3). pp. 414.

Chapter 10

- Anon., n.d. *Books.google.co.uk.* [Online]
  Available at: https://books.google.co.uk/books?id=7OmCBwAAQBAJ&pg=PT257&lpg=PT257&dq=All+parts+of+the+body+which+have+a+function,+if+used+in+moderation+and+exercised+in+labours+to+which+each+is+accustomed,+thereby+become+healthy+and+well%E2%80%93developed,+and+age+slow
  [Accessed 23 09 2015].

- Anon., n.d. *Heart.org.* [Online]
  Available at: http://www.heart.org/HEARTORG/GettingHealthy/PhysicalActivity/FitnessBasics/American-Heart-Association -Recommendations-for-Physical-Activity-in-Adults_UCM_307976_Article.jsp#.Vi_3v37hDIU
  [Accessed 08 08 2015].

- Anon., n.d. *Heath.harvard.edu.* [Online]
  Available at: http://www.health.harvard.edu/blog/regular-exercise-changes-brain-improve-memory-thinking-skills-201404097110
  [Accessed 09 08 2015].

- Anon., n.d. *NHS.uk.* [Online]
  Available at: http://www.nhs.uk/Livewell/fitness/Pages/physical-

BIBLIOGRAPHY

activity-guidelines-for-adults.aspx
[Accessed 07 07 2015].

- Anon., n.d. *Pinrest.com*. [Online]
Available at: https://www.pinterest.com/whitefield95/fitness/
[Accessed 09 09 2015].

- Anon., n.d. *WHO.int*. [Online]
Available at: http://www.who.int/about/definition/en/print.html
[Accessed 28 09 2015].

Chapter 11

- Anon., n.d. *Anxietyuk.org.uk*. [Online]
Available at: https://www.anxietyuk.org.uk/page/34/?ifs=1
[Accessed 29 09 2015].

- Anon., n.d. *APA.org*. [Online]
Available at: http://www.apa.org/helpcenter/understanding-psychotherapy.aspx
[Accessed 19 09 2015].

- Anon., n.d. *Brain y quote.com*. [Online]
Available at: http://www.brainyquote.com/quotes/quotes/m/marcusgarv381593.html
[Accessed 02 09 2015].

- Anon., n.d. *Helpguide.org*. [Online]
Available at: http://www.helpguide.org/articles/anxiety/therapy-for-anxiety-disorders.htm

- Anon., n.d. *IAPT* [Online]
Available at:
"http://www.nhs.uk/ServiceSearch/Psychological%20therapies%20(IAPT)/LocationSearch/10008"

- Borkovec, T. D., 1993. Efficacy Of Applied Relaxatation And Cognitive-Behavioral Therapy In The Treatment Of Generalized Anxiety Disorder. *Journal Consult Clin Psychology,* Volume 61, pp. 611-619.

- Bryant, R. A., 1998. Treatment of Acute Stress Disorder: A Comparison of Cognitive-Behavioral Therapy and Supportive Counseling. *Journal Clin. Psychology,* pp. 862-866.

- Bryant, R. A., 2005. The Audditive Benefit of Hypnosis and Cognitive-Behavioral Therapy in Treating Acute Stress Disorder. *Jorn. Consult Clin. Psychology,* Volume 73, pp. 334-340.

- Bryant, R. S., 1999. Treating Acute Stress Disorder: An Evaluation of Cognitive Behavior Therapy and Supportive Counseling Thechnique. *Amer. Journal Psychiatry,* Volume 156, pp. 1780-1786.

- Butler, A. C., 2005. The Empirical Status of Cognitive- Behavioral Theory: A Review of Meta- Analyses. *Clinical Psychology Review ,* 26(1), pp. 17-31.

- Weisz, J. R. D., 2006. Evidence-Based Youth Psychotherapies Versus Usual Clinical Care: A Meta- Analysis of Direct Comparison. *Am Psychol,* pp. 671-689.

Chapter 12

- Anon., n.d. *BAP.org.uk:.* [Online]
  Available at: http://www.bap.org.uk/pdfs/AnxietyGuidelines2014.pdf
  [Accessed 10 10 2015].
- Anon., n.d. *Emedmd.com.* [Online]
  Available at: www.emedmd.com/content/medication-anxiety
  [Accessed 11 11 2015].
- Anon., n.d. *Heath Harvard.edu.* [Online]
  Available at: http://health.harvard.edu/newsletter_article/when-depression-starts-in-the-neck
  [Accessed 15 11 2015].
- Anon., n.d. *Life Hack.org.* [Online]
  Available at: http://www.lifehack.org/articles/communication/when-you-face-difficult-times-kno
  [Accessed 23 09 2015].
- Anon., n.d. *Nice.org.uk:.* [Online]
  Available at: www.nice.org.uk/advice/KTT8
  [Accessed 20 10 2015].
- Chisholm, D. P., 2003. Depression Status, Medical Comorbidity and Resources Cost. Evidence from an International Study of Major Depression in Primary Care (LIDO). *BR J. Psychiatry,* 183(2), pp. 121-131.
- Fava, G. A., 2011. The Mechanisms of Tolerance in Antidepressant Action. *Prog Neuropsycholopharmacol Bio Psychiatry,* 35(7), pp. 1593-1602.
- Healy, D., 1997. *The Antidepressant Era.* Cambridge, Ma: Harvard University Press.
- Insel, T. R., 2009. The Star* D Trial: Revealing the Need for better Treatments. *Psychoatr Serv,* 60(11), pp. 1466-1467.
- Kirsch, I. D.-M., 2008. Initial Severity and Antidepressant Benefits: A Meta-Analysis of Data Submitted to the Food and Drug Administration. *PLoS Med ,* 5(2), p. 45.
- Van Praag, H., 2010. No Functional Psychopharmacology Without Functional Psychopathology. *Acta Psychiatr Scan,* 122(6), pp. 438-439.

Chapter 13

- Anon., n.d. *Azquotes.com.* [Online]
  Available at: http://www.azquotes.com/quote/1422463
  [Accessed 01 07 2015].
- Anon., n.d. *Book Mark Quotes.com.* [Online]

BIBLIOGRAPHY

- Available at: http://www.bookmarkquotes.com/view/i-think-any-breakup-from-long-relationship-has-this-accompanying-feeling-who-am-i-without-this-person-you-feel-like-halfperson-because-youve-greta-gerwig-77756.
  [Accessed 01 03 2016].

- Anon., n.d. *Cruse.org.uk.* [Online]
  Available at: http://www.cruse.org.uk/sites/default/files/default_images/pdf/Events/ColinMPcomplicatedgrief.pdf
  [Accessed 01 07 2015].

- Anon., n.d. *Google.com.* [Online]
  Available at: https://www.google.com.br/search?q=great+quotes&biw=1366&bih=643&source=lnms&tbm=isch&sa=X&ved=0CAYQ_AUoAWoVChMI35Ttm7b_yAIVxcMUCh3TEQeX#tbm=isch&q=graef+quotes&imgrc=Ab_dXaFO8sqOZM%3A
  [Accessed 27 07 2015].

- Anon., n.d. *Journey of Hearts.org.* [Online]
  Available at: http://www.journeyofhearts.org/grief/accident2.html
  [Accessed 13 08 2105].

- Anon., n.d. *Psychology Today.com.* [Online]
  Available at: Psycholwww.psychologytoday.com/blog/get-hardy/201309/about-complicated-bereavement-disorder-0
  [Accessed 27 09 2015].

- Anon., n.d. *Sistahfriends.com:.* [Online]
  Available at: http://sistahfriends.com/pages/Grief___Loss
  [Accessed 12 09 2015].

- Anon., n.d. *Sonoma.edu:.* [Online]
  Available at: https://www.sonoma.edu/users/d/daniels/lynch.html
  [Accessed 08 12 2015].

- Anon., n.d. *Stjh.org.uk:.* [Online]
  Available at: HYPERLINK "http://www.stjh.org.uk/neighbours" \h http://www.stjh.org.uk/neighbours
  [Accessed 08 12 2015].

Chapter 14

- Anon., n.d. *Azquotes.com.* [Online]
  Available at: http://www.azquotes.com/quote/620835
  [Accessed 10 02 2016].

- Anon., n.d. *Azquotes.com.* [Online]
  Available at: http://www.azquotes.com/quote/358920
  [Accessed 31 03 2016].

- Anon., n.d. *Azquotes.com.* [Online]
  Available at: http://www.azquotes.com/quote/890555
  [Accessed 29 03 2016].

- Anon., n.d. *Board of Wisdom.com.* [Online]
  Available at: http://boardofwisdom.com/togo/?viewid=1005&listname=Truth#.Vv1laf

krLIU
[Accessed 30 03 2016].

- Anon., n.d. *Boardofwisdom.com.* [Online]
  Available at:
  http://boardofwisdom.com/togo/Quotes/ShowQuote/?msgid=328679#.Vv2RTPkrLIU
  [Accessed 30 03 2016].

- Anon., n.d. *Brain Pickings.org.* [Online]
  Available at: https://www.brainpickings.org/2015/05/25/emerson-essays-lectures-experience/

- Anon., n.d. *Brainyquote.com.* [Online]
  Available at:
  http://www.brainyquote.com/quotes/quotes/j/jimrohn121282.html
  [Accessed 30 03 2016].

- Anon., n.d. *Brianmarkweller.wordpress.com.* [Online]
  Available at: https://brianmarkweller.wordpress.com/tag/jesus-christ/
  [Accessed 30 03 2016].

- Anon., n.d. *Icraved.wordpress.com.* [Online]
  Available at: https://icraved.wordpress.com/tag/looking-after-yourself/
  [Accessed 31 03 2016].

- Anon., n.d. *Lifehack.org.* [Online]
  Available at: http://www.lifehack.org/articles/communication/music-touches-emotionally-where-words-alone-cant.html
  [Accessed 31 03 2016].

- Anon., n.d. *Paulritchieblog.blogspot.co.uk.* [Online]
  Available at: http://paulritchieblog.blogspot.co.uk/2015/09/the-cross-should-be-our-measure-of-love.html
  [Accessed 28 03 2016].

- Anon., n.d. *Pictures.agodman.com.* [Online]
  Available at: http://pictures.agodman.com/bible-verses/john-832-and-you-shall-know-the-truth-and-the-truth-shall-set-you-free/
  [Accessed 29 03 2016].

- Anon., n.d. *Quotefancy.com.* [Online]
  Available at: https://quotefancy.com/quote/34224/Pablo-Picasso-The-meaning-of-life-is-to-find-your-gift-The-purpose-of-life-is-to-give-it
  [Accessed 30 03 2016].

- Anon., n.d. *Quotefancy.com.* [Online]
  Available at: https://quotefancy.com/quote/53086/Dalai-Lama-XIV-Do-not-let-the-behavior-of-others-destroy-your-inner-peace
  [Accessed 29 03 2016].

- Anon., n.d. *Quotepixel.com.* [Online]
  Available at: http://quotepixel.com/picture/friendship/page/10
  [Accessed 30 03 2016].

- Anon., n.d. *Quotesgram.com.* [Online]
  Available at: http://quotesgram.com/quotes-about-saying-no/
  [Accessed 28 03 2016].

- Anon., n.d. *Quotesgram.com.* [Online]

BIBLIOGRAPHY

- Available at: http://quotesgram.com/quotes-about-learning-from-others/
  [Accessed 25 03 2016].

- Anon., n.d. *Quotesgram.com.* [Online]
  Available at: http://quotesgram.com/peace-with-yourself-quotes/
  [Accessed 31 03 2016].

- Anon., n.d. *Quotesgram.com.* [Online]
  Available at: http://quotesgram.com/dying-of-laughter-quotes/
  [Accessed 31 03 2016].

- Anon., n.d. *Quotestoday.club.* [Online]
  Available at: http://www.quotestoday.club/nelson-mandela-quotes-it-always-seems-impossible-until-its-done/nelson-mandela-quotes-it-always-seems-impossible-until-its-done-2
  [Accessed 30 03 2016].

- Anon., n.d. *Simplymejustbe.wordpress.com.* [Online]
  Available at: https://simplymejustbe.wordpress.com/tag/philosophy/
  [Accessed 28 03 2016].

- Anon., n.d. *Thelifecoach.com.* [Online]
  Available at: http://www.thelifecoach.com/1284/myths-keep-trapped-perfectionism-part-two/
  [Accessed 01 02 2016].

- Anon., n.d. *Uk.pinterest.com.* [Online]
  Available at: https://uk.pinterest.com/pin/65372632065718097/
  [Accessed 29 03 2016].

- Anon., n.d. *Verybestquotes.com.* [Online]
  Available at: http://www.verybestquotes.com/in-optimism-there-is-magic-positive-quotes/
  [Accessed 28 03 2016].

- Anon., n.d. *Your tango.com.* [Online]
  Available at: http://www.yourtango.com/2013190143/37-friendship-quotes-famous-inspirational-best-friends-sayings
  [Accessed 30 03 2016].

www.ingramcontent.com/pod-product-compliance
Lightning Source LLC
Chambersburg PA
CBHW051053160426
43193CB00010B/1173